the way we die now

SEAMUS O'MAHONY is a Consultant Gastroenterologist at Cork University Hospital. He
is associate editor for medical humanities of
the *Journal of the Royal College of Physicians
of Edinburgh*, and is a regular contributor to
the *Dublin Review of Books*.

the
way
we
die
now

SEAMUS
O'MAHONY

First published in the UK in 2016 by Head of Zeus Ltd

This paperback edition first published in 2017 by Head of Zeus Ltd

3 5 7 9 8 6 4 2

A catalogue record for this book is available
from the British Library.

ISBN (PB) 9781784974282
ISBN (E) 9781784974251

Typeset by Adrian McLaughlin

Printed and bound by CPI Group (UK) Ltd,
Croydon, CR0 4YY

Head of Zeus Ltd
First Floor East
5–8 Hardwick Street
London EC1R 4RG

WWW.HEADOFZEUS.COM

This book is dedicated to the memory of
Dean Denis O'Connor (1922–2013) and
Tom Watret (1938–2013)

Contents

Prologue

Death, for most people, is a rumour; something that happens to others, far away. But it is the last thing you will 'do' – or which will happen to you – and the likelihood is that it will take place in an acute hospital or a care home, orchestrated by strangers. You will have little say in its pace or its manner. There is a risk that, during the course of your dying, you will be subjected to procedures and treatments that are painful, degrading and ultimately futile. If you are old, your children may make all the major decisions for you. Death may creep up on you without warning, without a chance for you to prepare yourself and settle your affairs.

Few books, as R.D. Laing remarked, are forgivable. Most of what I read about death and dying bears little relation to what I see every day in my work on the hospital wards. Doctors and nurses rarely write about death; those who do are generally palliative care (hospice) specialists, and have a particular perspective on the subject, one that

I do not completely share. The language used about death and dying tends to have a quality of cloying earnestness: nobody 'dies' anymore; they 'pass over', they 'pass on', or they simply 'pass'. The book I wanted to read about death and dying didn't exist.

Doctors who work in large, acute-care hospitals see death differently to doctors working in the hushed and serene environs of a hospice. And yet most dying still takes place in this kind of hospital, rather than in the hospices. Half a million people die every year in England. A study of deaths in England between 2005 and 2007 found that 58 per cent of all deaths occurred in hospital, 16 per cent in nursing homes, 19 per cent at home and only 5 per cent in hospices. The Irish figures are broadly similar: 48 per cent in hospital, 4 per cent in hospices. The agonizing decisions about whether to continue aggressive medical treatment of dying patients are taken by doctors like me. By the time the hospice doctors become involved, much of the heavy lifting has been done. The conversation about death and dying needs to be reclaimed: death is too important to be left to the death specialists.

No doubt a palliative care physician would have written a different book, but their patients are, if I may use the term, more 'packaged'. I deal with death in many guises: from the rapid and messy death in the emergency department resuscitation room, to the slow, painful death from liver disease on the general ward, to the high-tech, 'digital' death in the Intensive Care Unit (ICU). I am witness to the sudden deceleration in medical intensity, when we abruptly shift from full intervention to the side-room, the syringe-driver (which delivers a steady dose of morphine and sedative into the blood stream) and the chaplaincy service. The deaths I see are frequently undignified; the dying very often have not accepted or understood their situation, the truth denied them by well-intentioned relatives and doctors. Their death has been stolen from them.

But this is not a medical treatise. My interest may have been kindled by professional issues, but my scope is broader than that. My interest is as much personal as professional. Like most people, I am frightened of death – and medicine, apparently, attracts people with high personal anxieties about dying. The decline in religious belief in the West has exacerbated this fear. And, like many, I am haunted by a suspicion that our age, for all its technological and social progress, is one of spiritual poverty. We have paid a high price for our modern comforts.

This book has modest ambitions and is the product of my own experiences, reading and (I dare say) prejud-ices. Although I am Irish by birth, and work in Ireland, I am not writing specifically about death and dying in Ireland. Whilst every country has its own legal and cultural microclimate, what I have to say applies, I hope, to developed countries in general. I do, however, deal with some specifically British controversies, namely, the

Stafford scandal and the Liverpool Care Pathway, because their stories tell us much about modern death and dying.

I will try to explain why modern acute hospitals make a good death increasingly difficult, and will contrast the experience in the general hospitals with that in hospices. I will examine the historical and societal factors which led to the 'hidden death', and why we are so fearful of honesty in our dealings with death and the dying – what the late Kieran Sweeney called a 'hesitation to be brave'. I believe that much of modern medicine is characterized by a culture of excess and dishonesty, and this culture ill-serves the dying.

I will examine contemporary ideas about death from cancer by looking at the stories of Christopher Hitchens, Susan Sontag, Josephine Hart and Nuala O'Faolain. I will show how modern medicine and society at large have conspired to banish death from our consciousness, or at least to sanitize it, and how this has led to bizarre modern fantasies about immortality. I hope to persuade you that our obsession with controlling the timing and manner of our death, with advance directives and legally sanctioned assisted suicide, is ultimately self-defeating. I had previously assumed that a 'philosophical' attitude helped people die better, but found that this assumption did not bear close scrutiny. This is not a book of consolation: death is simply affliction and the end of our days. We are frail and vulnerable animals.

CHAPTER 1

What Do I Know?

We used to have a common script for dying. The great French historian Philippe Ariès coined the term 'tame death' to describe the way people died in Europe during the thousand years before the Industrial Revolution. Death was feared and regarded as a blow to the community, but the dying and their attendants knew how to *do* it. Death was familiar, death was swift, death was acknowledged and death was public. When death was no longer 'tame', when it became hidden and medicalized, we found ourselves lost and disorientated, without a script to follow. We have banished death so comprehensively from our thoughts that one of the most famous artworks of the last twenty-five years, Damien Hirst's shark-in-a-tank-of-formaldehyde, is pithily entitled 'The Physical Impossibility of Death in the Mind of Someone Living'. This is a modern take on Freud's aphorism: 'It is indeed impossible to imagine our own death; and whenever we attempt to do so, we can perceive that we are in fact still present as spectators.'

We have been forced to write our own script. Illness memoirs and blogs written by the dying have a popular appeal because people want to know how to compose this script. There is, however, something studied and self-congratulatory – even narcissistic – about all this, as there is with the modern clamour for 'death with dignity'. I recall that when my children were born in the mid-1990s, I used to joke that we, the new parents, with our childbirth classes and nappy-changing fathers, behaved as if we were the first generation ever to have babies. I sometimes feel the same about contemporary approaches to death. We're the first generation to 'do' death on our terms. We are blogging, penning memoirs and newspaper columns. Those dying young enough to understand social media are dying online: there is a cacophony of voices, a thousand scripts you can choose from. Memorial sites to the dead appear on Facebook, where they are known as electronic graves. But how much of this stuff is read by those who live in the Kingdom of the Well?

Those well-intentioned and earnest folk who write and lecture about death and dying hold up the 'good death' and 'death with dignity' as their ideal. I support their desire to treat pain properly and to protect the dying from futile treatments. But I sometimes wonder if what they want is to re-tame death, in a modern way: to strip it of its awesome grandeur, to turn it into a process that can be managed, policed, workshopped – the care of the dying man reduced to trite formulas. Philippe Ariès wrote in the early 1970s:

> A small elite proposes not so much to 'evacuate' death as to humanize it. They acknowledge the necessity of death, but they want it to be accepted and no longer shameful... They propose to reconcile death with happiness. Death must become the discreet but dignified exit of a peaceful person from a helpful society that is not torn, not even overly upset by the idea of a biological transition without significance, without pain or suffering, and ultimately without fear.

Henry James called it 'the distinguished thing', but death, for most people, is banal, anti-climactic. The End is robbed of its significance by our new hospital rituals. Most people who die in the hospital where I work do so after several days of syringe-driver-induced oblivion. As in most other momentous events of human life, the professionals have taken over. Ivan Illich, that turbulent priest and philosopher, argued that dying was yet another aspect of human life which had been colonized and taken over by medical busybodies. We need to reclaim death from the experts, to make awareness of it part of our everyday lives, to de-medicalize it, or, at least, to reduce over-medicalization. I do not suggest that we can magically rid ourselves of the fear of it, or that we should try obsessively to control the manner and timing of it. Death is grand and mysterious. It cannot be hidden away; the doing of it should not be reduced to a set of tried and tested manoeuvres.

GROWING UP AROUND DEATH

Cork, in the south of Ireland, 1972 – I was twelve years old. My mother woke me very early, maybe at 5 or 6 o'clock. She told me that a neighbour, a boy of twenty-one, had been killed in a car crash. His parents could not face the visit to the morgue to identify the body, and this task was delegated to my father, who was a close friend. I attended the funeral with my parents; my two younger brothers were left at home. The coffin was open. His battered face was still handsome, but even I could see the undertaker's work. Grown men were weeping. There was no consolation, only anguish. His mother mourned him for another forty-two years, the last ten in the mist of dementia. She went on to bury two more of her five children. One of the unexpected benefits of dementia was her belief that her favourite son was still alive. She died at ninety.

My mother's close friend M. gave birth to a baby boy around the same time I was born. They were in the same ward in the maternity hospital. After a series of chest infections during infancy, the boy was eventually diagnosed with cystic fibrosis. In the 1960s, children afflicted with this condition rarely survived beyond their teens. The boy didn't live to be a teenager. M. still sends me a card for the big birthdays; my milestones a reminder of her lost child.

Essex, 1980 – I had a summer job, working as a nursing assistant on a geriatric ward in a run-down hospital on the outskirts of London. The ward staff were a mixture of the good and the not-so-good, the hard-working and the lazy, and the patients were given as much comfort and care as the circumstances allowed. The ward sister was a genial, slightly mocking lady, who would often give me a gin and tonic after a particularly hard shift. The doctors attended infrequently, and showed little interest. The consultant appeared perhaps once a week, and was guided quickly around by the sister, who made sure he took no big decisions. Most of my patients were elderly men with dementia. My job was to get them up, wash and shave them, and feed them, a truly Sisyphean task. It was a good experience for me, but a miserable life for my patients.

I noticed that dementia took different forms. One man

retained a degree of insight into his affliction. He put a great deal of effort into his appearance: he was 'dapper', in the way that working-class men of his era were. His hair was brillantined, he had a little pencil moustache, and wore a silk dressing-gown. He maintained a public carapace of jaunty, cockney cheerfulness: 'Musn't grumble!' He had lost one of his legs (below the knee) to smoking-related peripheral vascular disease, so he was prone to falling. Longing for death, he died after a fall. He had no visitors.

Another of my men told me the same story every day: he had been a driver for the British army during the war, and on one occasion he had driven Winston Churchill and King George VI. His eyes would fill with tears as he recalled it: 'The King of England and the greatest Englishman what ever lived!'

My oldest patient, Tom, had fought in the Somme: you could still feel the copper wire that had been used in the field hospital to bind his shattered knee. His only remaining pleasure was smoking, although he did enjoy the sensation of being shaved. In those days, smoking was allowed on the wards, and one of my jobs was to roll his cigarettes and light them for him. I fed him slowly, spoon by spoon, much of which he spat out. This task created a strange, intimate bond between feeder and patient: if he was in a good mood, he called me 'good old boy'; if he wasn't, he called me a 'fucking c***'. Because he was somewhat deaf, the only way I could communicate with him was to affect a cockney accent. He was indifferent as to whether he lived or died. He had a large and devoted family, who visited frequently, and spoke to me every day about him. They were stunned by the decline of their patriarch. He died one night in his sleep; I was off-duty and learned the news when I came in for the early shift. It was imparted by the ward sister with her usual note of rueful, slightly indifferent, resignation. There was some discussion, I recall, about how the copper wire in his knee would cause problems with cremation.

An elderly retired doctor lived with his wife in an annexe of the nurses' home. He had worked for many years as resident medical officer at the hospital, never climbing any higher on the career ladder. He liked to chat with me and my two classmates who had come with me to work in the hospital. He boasted one evening, in his cups, of killing off many 'hopeless cases' by injecting them with large doses of morphine: 'Best thing for the poor buggers.' Harold Shipman, too, killed his patients with morphine, although this drug is not especially effective for the task: the Dignitas clinic in Switzerland, which knows a thing or two about killing people, does not use morphine.

Cork, 1984 – I was the Senior House Officer on call that day for General Medicine. The switchboard put through a call from my youngest brother, phoning from home. My father, aged seventy-one, had collapsed outside the house, while walking the dog. My brother called the ambulance. I dropped everything and drove the short distance home. The ambulance was just leaving when I arrived. My father was taken to the resuscitation room of the emergency department. I stood at the door, and watched the scene unfold. He was not breathing; a tube was inserted into his airway, and a team of junior doctors started giving him cardiac massage. It wasn't working. I indicated to them that they should stop, and they were happy to comply. Had my brother not called me, I would have been a member of this Cardiac Arrest Team, running down to the resuscitation room, not knowing whom I was going to be faced with.

Sudden, premature death was common among the men on the street where I grew up. R. – a few doors up – dropped dead, aged forty, leaving a wife and six children. S. – two doors down – died of a heart attack, aged sixty, leaving five children. D. – three doors up – at the age of fifty, collapsed, and died of a ruptured abdominal aneurysm in the ambulance. My mother still lives – alone – in the same street; many of the houses are now occupied by widows.

DOING DEATH FOR A LIVING

I have worked as a doctor for more than thirty years, nearly all that time spent in large, acute hospitals.

Death in modern hospitals still has the faint whiff of an industrial accident, a failure of medical intervention. When I was a student, treatment of the dying was briefly and fleetingly covered – death being a 'negative outcome'. We – the medical profession – had begun to believe in the delusion that we could tame nature, that all illnesses were potentially curable. Yet death was all around – in the wards, in the resuscitation room, in the morgue.

In those days, before the scandals about organ retention, many, if not most people dying in hospitals underwent a post-mortem examination. When I was a medical student, we were required to attend at least twenty post-mortems. These were surprisingly sociable events, with a large crowd of jostling students nervously and obligingly laughing at the pathologist's jokes. The process involved in dissecting a corpse to establish the cause of death is indescribably gruesome, and I thought at the time that no family would consent to such a procedure if they could witness what actually goes on. I watched as the lungs, upper airway and tongue were removed in one piece. I saw how the skull was opened with a drill to extract the brain. I saw the bodies of dead babies and old ladies and young suicides. I had fallen behind in my attendance, and towards the end of the year there was a serious risk that I would not reach the required minimum of twenty. I was friendly with one of the pathology registrars, who would let me sit in on post-mortems at weekends, so I sometimes saw several on a single visit.

I should add that post-mortems were not as shocking for us medical students as they might have been because we had experience of the dissection room. The first visit to this room was, I admit, disconcerting: the overpowering smell of formaldehyde, the waxy, almost unreal corpses. We learned very little of lasting value over the two years spent carrying out dissections in the anatomy department, and I felt guilty that the public-spirited volunteers had donated their bodies for so little benefit.

During my first three years as a doctor, I was regularly part of the cardiac arrest team when I was on-call at nights and weekends. This showed me death in the raw, chiefly because cardio-pulmonary resuscitation was then (and still is) so spectacularly unsuccessful. Very often, we were 'bagging' with oxygen and cardiac-massaging people who were well and truly dead, the team called only to keep up appearances. It was not unknown for a nurse, having found a patient dead in their bed in the middle of the night, to call the arrest team, thus giving the impression to the relatives that she had chanced upon the patient just at the moment when they stopped breathing and had acted with the utmost diligence and initiative. Perhaps the most bizarre arrest call was to attend a patient who had jumped to his death from the top floor of the hospital, down to the concrete below. His mangled body was beyond fixing.

I was struck on more than one occasion by the sheer terror of those few still conscious near the end. One man has stayed in my memory. It was a Saturday afternoon in Bradford Royal Infirmary, Yorkshire, sometime in the mid-1990s. I was senior registrar on call for General Medicine, and was summoned to see a man in the Coronary Care Unit. He was in his mid-fifties, admitted to the unit with a myocardial infarction (heart attack). He had severe chest pain and breathlessness. I gave him an injection of morphine, but it didn't work, and he looked at me with a twisted rictus of fear, the physical expression of pure horror. His heart stopped beating and we failed to resuscitate him. He died, his last conscious sensations being those of pain, the struggle for breath as he drowned in his own bodily fluid, and terror. The deathbed was the usual scene of a blue and battered corpse, oozing blood from all the punctured arteries and veins, surrounded by empty syringes, blood-stained sheets, and a silent arrest team.

Another man haunts me too: in his forties, he was admitted with a flare-up of his asthma. The arrest team (of which I was the most junior member) was called because he had suddenly become extremely short of breath. When we arrived on the ward, the man was blue and gasping for air. We didn't know what was causing this. He was given oxygen, but did not improve, and stopped breathing completely. The most senior member of the team, the medical registrar, tried to intubate him, but instead of placing the tube in his trachea (windpipe), he placed it in the oesophagus (gullet), which resulted in a violent expulsion of vomitus. By the time the anaesthetics registrar arrived, he was beyond rescue. A post-mortem examination showed that he had a tension pneumothorax: the lung had suddenly collapsed. Not one of us had considered this as a possibility. Pneumothorax can be treated – relatively easily – by placing a drain in the chest cavity.

But life goes on, and after a few glasses of wine at home, you move on to the next day, the next awfulness. Doctors, unlike, say, soldiers or policemen, rarely admit to being affected by the horrors they have seen, and are seemingly immune to post-traumatic stress disorder.

THE FUTILE TUBE

Perhaps this immunity is partly owing to the fact that, although we see it every day, doctors do not think very much about death and dying. In my case, one of the reasons this became so was a procedure called percutaneous endoscopic gastrostomy (PEG). My specialism is gastro-enterology, and much of my work is performing endoscopic procedures. PEG is one such endoscopic procedure, which I first carried out in the early 1990s. It involves the placement of a feeding tube through the abdominal wall, directly into the stomach, bypassing the mouth and gullet. PEG tubes are commonly inserted in patients who cannot eat or swallow. Most of these patients are old and frail.

This procedure was first described by two US surgeons, Jeffrey Ponsky and Michael Gauderer in 1980, and was initially used mainly in children with severe neurological disability. After doing this procedure for some time, it gradually dawned on me that in most patients PEG was futile and potentially harmful. Many people with dementia were subjected to the procedure, despite the fact that several studies had shown that it did not prolong life, improve nutrition or prevent suffering. People who had sustained a severe, incapacitating stroke, with no prospect of recovery, were kept pitifully alive by it. There were lengthy and complex legal disputes revolving around PEG feeding of individuals with persistent vegetative state in Britain and in the US, in the respective cases of Tony Bland, who suffered severe brain injury during the Hillsborough disaster in 1989, and Terri Schiavo, who was left severely brain-damaged having been resuscitated after she had a cardiac arrest at home in 1990.

In 2002, I happened to be at the annual meeting of the American Gastroenterology Association in Atlanta. This meeting attracts up to 15,000 delegates from all over the world; the atmosphere is one of pomposity and hubris. At the end of a 'plenary' session on endoscopy, Jeffrey Ponsky was presented with an award, honouring his contribution to the speciality. Before the handing over of the actual award, we were treated to a short film about the great man. I learned that he was keen on horse-riding and country music, and that, way back in the 1960s, his mother-in-law had loaned him the money to buy endoscopes when he had a hunch that this would be the future. As I sat in the vast auditorium, I reflected that Jeffrey Ponsky's co-invention of PEG was not an unalloyed boon to humanity.

Over time, I became increasingly uncomfortable carrying out the insertion of these feeding tubes, and invested a lot of time and psychic energy in trying to dissuade families and well-meaning colleagues from authorizing the procedure. Eventually I reached the uncomfortable conclusion that, in most cases, this form of feeding was instituted mainly to meet the complex emotional, professional – even economic – needs of families and care-givers, rather than those of the patient. PEG, in many cases, was a technical panacea for existential problems.

This fact, of course, was unacknowledged, or was actively denied. It is much easier, for example, to feed elderly confused people by PEG than by the slow, laborious, sometimes frustrating and expensive (in terms of labour costs) method of spoon-feeding. PEG feeding is a superficially attractive solution to all forms of eating difficulties in the frail, the old and the dying, but comes at a high price, with the risk of the procedure itself, along with chronic problems of aspiration pneumonia, diarrhoea, tube leakage and infection. More importantly, it turns the ordinary human activity of eating into a medical intervention, and deprives people of this simple pleasure. I actively – and successfully – resisted pressure from other doctors to insert PEG tubes into the dying. The procedure became for me a symbol of the medicalization of death, and of the failure of modern medicine to care humanely for those most in need of its help.

Some years ago, I was asked by a neurologist colleague to insert a PEG tube in a woman with advanced motor neurone disease who had swallowing difficulties. The patient herself was ambivalent about having the procedure, but her husband was aggressively insistent. He had bullied both his wife and her consultant, and hovered outside the Endoscopy Unit when she came down from the ward to have the PEG tube inserted. He insisted that his wife was not competent to make decisions about her treatment, and announced that he would not leave until the PEG tube was inserted. I proceeded reluctantly, and – to my enduring shame – carried out the procedure, even after the woman said, 'I don't want this.'

One of the first tube insertions of this kind I carried out in the early 1990s was in a man with dementia. The procedure was straightforward and seemingly uncomplicated, but the following day he became suddenly unwell with severe abdominal pain and fever. He clearly had peritonitis, which usually means that an abdominal organ has been perforated. The surgeon on-call refused to operate, on the grounds that the man was so frail that an operation would kill him. He was therefore treated 'conservatively' with antibiotics and intravenous fluids, but died the next day. Because this man died following a medical procedure, the coroner was notified, and I was eventually called to give evidence at the inquest. A very distinguished forensic pathologist described the post-mortem findings. The end (the 'button') of the PEG tube was not where it should have been – in the stomach cavity – but outside the stomach, in the peritoneal cavity. When I had completed the procedure, I had checked that the 'button' was within the stomach, which it was. The overwhelmingly likely explanation was that this poor demented old man, in his confusion, had pulled the 'button' out of the stomach, but not out of the abdomen. The nurses did not notice this, and continued to feed him, with the liquid feed going directly into his peritoneum, not into the stomach. I often think about this man. Nowadays, he would never have had the procedure.

I recently came across an old thank-you note, from the four siblings of a patient who died many years ago, when I worked in the UK. R. was a woman in her late fifties, who had been in institutional care for many years. She had multiple disabilities, including cerebral palsy, with mild intellectual disability, diabetes and recurrent chest infections. I had first encountered R. a few years before that, when she was referred to me for a PEG tube insertion. I saw her at my clinic, where she arrived with a committee of carers, including nurses, a dietician, and a speech and language therapist. The speech and language therapist had carried out a detailed assessment of R.'s swallowing and had diagnosed a 'severe swallowing disorder', with a high risk of choking, which in turn could lead to aspiration of food into the lungs, causing pneumonia. She recommended that R. should have a PEG tube. I explained patiently that several studies had shown that PEG tubes, far from curing this problem, actually *increase* the risk of aspiration pneumonia. The committee expressed its collective displeasure and left the clinic unhappy.

Some days later, I took a call from R.'s sister. I was expecting trouble, but it turned out that she was a senior nurse and was calling to let me know that she agreed with my assessment. The family, however, were being put under intolerable pressure by the staff at R.'s care home. R. didn't want a PEG tube herself. Her ability to swallow was indeed poor, but she enjoyed her food and the sociability of mealtimes. Her mother, to whom she had been very close, had died a couple of years before, and R.'s zest for life had diminished gradually since then. In order to mollify the nurses at R.'s care home, I admitted her to the ward for a week or so, and we found that her food intake was just about sufficient for her needs. She went back to the home without a PEG tube. Over the next couple of years, R. had several admissions with chest infection, and one of these infections eventually killed her. I relate this story because in many ways it is so atypical. Peaceful and dignified death is hard to achieve in acute-care hospitals. Some relatives do not thank me for a non-interventionist approach; one family, in a similar clinical scenario, accused me of attempted euthanasia.

Although I am primarily a gastroenterologist, I also do a lot of what is known as 'general' medicine. When I am 'on take' for General Medicine, I accept everything that the super-specialists do not want. Most of these patients are frail and old, with multiple diseases. Many have dementia. I am ashamed to admit that I once viewed the care of such patients as unworthy of my attention as a highly specialized gastroenterologist. Many of these people were at the end of their lives and caring for them forced me to think about death and dying.

The majority of my really sick in-patients are those with liver failure caused by cirrhosis, mainly attributable to alcohol. I witnessed the death, on my first Christmas Day back in Ireland after fourteen years in the UK, of a twenty-seven-year-old boy – for a boy was all he was – with alcoholic liver disease. Since then, I have witnessed many such deaths, as Ireland shot from the bottom to the top of the European alcohol consumption league table. Mortality in these patients is worse than for most cancers, and death from liver failure can be particularly gruesome. The patients tend to be mainly young (in their thirties and forties) and most do not qualify for liver transplantation.

Some years ago, I was called on a Sunday afternoon by a surgical registrar at the hospital. I was not on-call, but he needed help with a liver cirrhosis patient, who was bleeding profusely from oesophageal varices (varicose veins in the gullet caused by cirrhosis). I drove into the hospital, taking my ten-year-old son with me, because my wife was away at the time. I left my son in my office and went to the operating theatre; I told him I would not be long. The patient, a man in his forties, was in a bad way: he was jaundiced, grotesquely swollen owing to fluid retention, and semi-comatose. We carried out an endoscopy to find (and, we hoped, to treat) the source of bleeding. As expected, the patient had oesophageal varices. We were unable to stop the bleeding, and over the next two hours struggled in vain to save him. Meanwhile, my son, locked in my office, wondered if he had been abandoned. Exhausted and bloody, I eventually collected him and drove home. On the drive back, I told him what had happened. He resolved there and then never to become a doctor.

I have witnessed so many deaths from liver failure in relatively young people. Yet death is rarely discussed as a possibility since patients and their families tend to assume that modern medicine can fix broken organs, or that if they cannot be fixed, they can be replaced. Although cirrhosis of the liver has a worse prognosis than most cancers, patients rarely get the type of palliative care available to people with cancer. They die after long and messy hospitalizations, the medical technology pushed right to the bitter end.

BAD NEWS

My daily work also caused me to think about cancer care. I regularly diagnose many common cancers, such as those of the colon, oesophagus, stomach, pancreas and liver. Although my main role is diagnosis, I also carry out treatments for cancer, such as inserting stents (tubes) in patients with jaundice as a result of bile duct obstruction caused by pancreatic, and bile-duct cancers. The most challenging part of my job with cancer patients, however, is giving the bad news. This job frequently falls to me, before the patient is seen by a cancer specialist – an oncologist. I believe it is unfair to expect an oncologist to see a patient without first telling that patient what an oncologist is, and why they need to see one.

One of the more pernicious myths of modern medicine is the notion that a doctor with 'communication skills' and a sympathetic manner can somehow magically transmute bad news into something palatable, that he or she can, Mary Poppins-like, give a spoonful of sugar to help the medicine go down. Medical students now attend workshops on 'How to Give Bad News'. This notion of managing Bad News is symptomatic of the temptation to rebrand the terrors we humans inevitably face – principally death – as almost some form of personal growth. Patients and relatives are said to be on a 'journey', and the rather speculative notions of Elisabeth Kübler-Ross on the emotional responses of dying people (the five stages of denial, anger, bargaining, depression and acceptance) are now trotted out, as if they were scientific fact. People react in all sorts of ways to their impending death, and I cannot recall a single person moving neatly through Kübler-Ross's five stages. The power and terror of death refuses to be tamed by workshops, by trite formulae. No more than life, can death be packaged and processed into bite-sized chunks. Death is always sovereign, always in control.

THE WHIPPING BOY

Relatives of dying people experience complex emotions. Doctors caring for the dying increasingly find themselves in conflict with patients' families, and over the years I have endured some bitter and unedifying battles. Many years ago, when I worked in the NHS, an elderly woman with dementia was admitted under my care. She arrived at the hospital with aspiration pneumonia, almost certainly the result of a PEG feeding tube inserted – unwisely, under pressure from the family – in another hospital. When her condition deteriorated, I tried to persuade her many children that intensive care treatment, which would involve intubation (insertion of a breathing tube) and mechanical ventilation, was not appropriate for a woman of her age with advanced dementia. Inevitably, however, she was admitted to the ICU over the following weekend, when I was not on-call, and the medical registrar came under intense pressure from the family to escalate the old lady's care. She was transferred from the general ward to the ICU, where she was intubated and ventilated and, rather miraculously, survived. On the Monday morning, along with one of the ICU consultants, I met the family and talked with them for over an hour. Again, we tried to persuade them that Intensive Care was too interventionist for their mother. One of the daughters angrily accused us of attempting euthanasia. Another daughter announced that she would take her mother to a private hospital, where she would be treated 'properly'. The meeting ended acrimoniously and unresolved. The ICU consultant stood his ground and told them that in the event of a further deterioration, the ICU would not admit her.

The old lady went back to the general ward, and lingered for several months. Over that time, I had many meetings with the family, along with regular correspondence from their solicitor and the hospital risk managers. The relationship between the family and the ward staff grew increasingly strained. The daughters constantly challenged the nurses and junior doctors and, on occasion, interfered with the electronic settings controlling the delivery of intravenous fluids and antibiotics to their mother. One of them took to writing instructions on the drug-chart, stating that her mother was not to be given morphine under any circumstances. As the situation deteriorated, a committee convened by the hospital's clinical director finally decided that the patient should be made a ward of court, so that the hospital would no longer be answerable to the family. While this legal process was getting under way, the old woman's condition suddenly deteriorated, and she died. Her death was farcical and undignified. Although I had made it clear to the family that we would not attempt cardio-pulmonary resuscitation, when the poor woman finally died, two of the daughters attempted their own cack-handed version of cardiac massage and mouth-to-mouth resuscitation.

Around the same time, a woman in her forties with liver failure, caused by alcoholic cirrhosis, was admitted under my care, and I endured a similarly bitter and unedifying conflict with her brother and sister. She eventually died after enduring a long, painful series of setbacks and complications over six months. She was not a candidate for liver transplantation, but I failed to persuade her family that this was so. A second opinion was asked for and provided, only for the patient's sister to accuse me of unduly influencing the doctor (a liver transplant specialist) who gave this second opinion. I requested a third opinion, which concurred with both my assessment and the second opinion. Again, a great deal of correspondence passed between solicitors and hospital risk managers.

Her sister, a successful lawyer, tended to visit the ward late in the evenings and demand an update on her sister's blood tests – the more obscure and clinically irrelevant, the more she agitated. The nurses and junior doctors were terrified of her. I met this sister on many occasions in an attempt to mollify her, but it became clear to me after several of these meetings that I was making no progress. After one bitter weekend, when this sister created mayhem on the ward, I refused to engage in any further discussions with her and dealt with her younger brother instead. The brother, unfortunately, simply passed on his elder sister's instructions and demands. I tried to engage openly and honestly with the patient herself about the problems we were having with her sister, but she continued to defer to her elder sibling in all matters. I tried, in vain, to persuade her to see the palliative care services. She died slowly and painfully, over six months, in an atmosphere of conflict and denial.

Shortly after her death, I learned something about the complex family dynamic from her brother, who finally broke rank. My patient, who was single, had given up her job when her elderly mother became ill and could not look after herself. She cared for her mother for several years. When the old woman finally died, my patient was left alone, without a job or a purpose. Alcohol filled the void. Her difficult sister, who had married and prospered, seemingly channelled her free-floating guilt into conflict with doctors and nurses.

TWO DEATHS

My elderly uncle, a much-loved priest, was sick throughout 2012. It had all started with a minor stroke. Although the stroke affected his balance, he insisted on going home before his doctor felt he was ready. A few days later, he fell in the kitchen and fractured his hip. I went to the Emergency Department that evening, and found him in great pain. The surgeons had to delay doing hip-replacement surgery because my uncle had emphysema and heart disease, and they wanted to get him as fit as possible for the procedure. He eventually had the operation, but then endured a series of setbacks, including a bowel obstruction, for which he had a second operation. He spent several months in hospital. His appetite was

poor, and he tended to cough and splutter when he ate.
Already frail, he lost weight. The speech and language
therapists predictably recommended a PEG tube, but he
wisely declined. His many parishioners were devoted to
him, but the constant stream of visitors exhausted him.
Often I had to ask them to leave.

It became clear that my uncle would never be well
enough to go home and a place was found for him in a
nursing home run by an order of nuns. By now he was
breathless even at rest, and could walk only a few steps with
the aid of a frame. He had as many visitors as ever, and said
daily mass in the chapel of the nursing home. His many
nieces and nephews took it in turns to take him out, but
these excursions became increasingly exhausting for him.
One of the last outings was to my house, to celebrate my
mother's eightieth birthday. I invited all of his extended
family: he had christened and married all of us. We knew
it would be the last time we would be together with him. In
December, he reached his ninetieth birthday, an occasion
he declined to celebrate. Late in February 2013, he
developed pneumonia and was sent back to the hospital.
He had no reserves to combat it, and died a week later.

The year 2012 ended with the news that my father-in-law
had a malignant tumour of his bone, chondrosarcoma.
He was seventy-four and, before then, had enjoyed
excellent health. He was slim; played golf several times a

week; had never smoked. He had complained for several weeks of an ache in his left thigh. He phoned me for advice and I suggested he visit his GP with a view to getting an X-ray. The X-ray showed something abnormal in the shaft of the femur, the thigh-bone. I knew this wasn't good. Things then moved fast: he was admitted to his local hospital in Dumfries, in the south-west of Scotland, and had a scan, which showed a large bone tumour. The local orthopaedic surgeons arranged for him to have further treatment at a specialist bone cancer unit in Glasgow. In the interim he was sent home, and given a combination of painkilling drugs. He felt ghastly; a few days later, an ambulance took him to Glasgow. When he arrived there, he experienced excruciating pain in his thigh getting into the hospital bed. The doctors in Glasgow discovered that he had developed a degree of kidney failure, caused by the painkilling drugs, and that his thigh-bone had fractured at the site of the tumour – a 'pathological' fracture – an indicator, I knew, of a poor prognosis.

He underwent major surgery, although there was some suspicion before the operation that the tumour had spread to his lungs. The operation removed most of his thigh-bone, replacing it with a metal rod. The recovery was slow and painful. Pathological analysis of the tumour showed that it was 'high-grade', that is, highly malignant. I phoned his surgeon, who was polite and circumspect, but who left me in little doubt about the bleak prognosis. My father-in-law was sent back to the hospital in Dumfries for physiotherapy and rehabilitation to get him back on his feet. He was discharged on Christmas Eve; his arrival home by ambulance was joyous and tearful.

A month later, he went back to Glasgow to see an oncologist, who told him that chemotherapy or radiation treatment had nothing to offer. Back at home, he gamely did his exercises and his physiotherapy, but continued to require crutches. His thigh became increasingly painful; he was advised that this was just normal post-operative swelling and was to be expected. After several months during which he endured increasing pain and swelling, a scan revealed local recurrence of the tumour in his thigh, along with a large blood clot. Shortly after, another scan confirmed the presence of tumour in his lungs. Thereafter – unsurprisingly – he gave up the exercises.

GOOD DEATH, BAD DEATH

These days, we hear the phrase 'a good death' bandied about. So what constitutes the ideal death? Naturally, we want it to be free of pain. Most of us want it to happen at home, in an atmosphere of dignity and calm, surrounded by family. Our contemporary culture values the idea of death as 'personal growth', a spiritual event:

those attending the dying should feel privileged. A 'good death' is also one where the dying man and his family and friends openly acknowledge its imminence. Death is also an opportunity for 'closure', when conflicts and unfinished business are resolved.

So the contemporary consensus is that it should go something like this: at the age of one hundred, after a lifetime of professional achievement and personal happiness, you become acutely ill, having never experienced any sickness more serious than a cold. This illness does not rob you of your mental faculties, your ability to communicate or to enjoy food. The nature of this disease allows your medical attendants to predict with pinpoint accuracy the hour of your demise. You gather your family and friends to tell them how much you've enjoyed your life, and how much you love them all. You make practical arrangements for your property and business interests. If you are religious, you receive the last rites and make peace with your God. You are able to distil and pass on the wisdom accrued over your long life. You eat one last, delicious, meal. You raise your hand and say 'Goodbye'. You close your eyes, and die immediately. Your family and friends, though distraught by your leaving, undergo a powerful spiritual experience. Your life and example has enriched their lives. Your funeral is an occasion of joy and renewal, attended by thousands. You will live forever in the memory of those you have left behind.

We know, of course, that dying isn't like that at all. You are likely to die after a long, chronic illness. This illness may rob you of your mind and your ability to communicate: dying dismantles not only the body, but frequently the spirit too. It is highly probable that you will depend on others to help carry out ordinary bodily functions (eating, dressing, going to the toilet). This death is most likely to happen in a general hospital or a nursing home. It is much less likely to happen in your own bed at home, and even less likely again to take place in a hospice. It will probably happen with strangers in attendance. The end will be sudden and precipitate, after a long decline. You may not be aware that you are dying, so you may not get the chance to say goodbye properly to family and friends. Near the end, over the last few days, it is highly likely that you will be unconscious, sedated and pain-free on a syringe-driver. The syringe-driver may be linked up before you even realize you are dying. The pleasure of food and drink will be a distant memory, as will all other pleasures. You may withdraw from others towards the end, as dying animals do, and turn to the wall, as dying humans have done for millennia.

CHAPTER 2

Hidden Death

In the mid-1960s, cultural commentators in Europe and North America began to write about how death had become something to be spoken of in hushed whispers, something to be covered up, hidden, even denied. There were many reasons for this: the rapid advances in scientific medicine, industrialization, the loosening of the bonds that held together traditional communities, the decline in religious belief. Parallel with this new death-taboo, these commentators observed a growing concern that death in modern hospitals was becoming more technical, more 'undignified'. Four authors in particular – two anthropologists, a social philosopher and a historian – wrote about this phenomenon. The four, Philippe Ariès (a Frenchman), Geoffrey Gorer (an Englishman), Ernest Becker (an American) and Ivan Illich (an Austrian), were all essentially loners. Their backgrounds, literary styles and influences were vastly different, but they all concluded that something profound had happened in the twentieth century to human beings' relationship with their own mortality.

PHILIPPE ARIÈS:
TAME DEATH, HIDDEN DEATH

There is something singularly admirable about the French historian Philippe Ariès (1914–84), who toiled away for years on his huge *opera*, assisted only by his wife and sustained by bloody-mindedness and a passion for his subject. He was born in Blois, in the Loire Valley, south-west of Orléans, to a devoutly Catholic and royalist family. After taking his primary degree at the University of Grenoble, he studied history as a graduate student at the Sorbonne, but became disillusioned with academic life and did not take his post-graduate degree or pursue a career as a professional historian. He supported himself by working in business (tropical fruit), but continued his historical work: fittingly, his memoir is called *Un Historien du dimanche* ('A Sunday Historian') (1980).

As a student, Ariès had become disenchanted with

orthodox narrative history, which seemed to concern itself mainly with great wars and political events. Instead, he became a 'social' or 'cultural' historian and wrote history through the prism of ordinary lives. His first great achievement was *L'Enfant et la vie familiale sous l'ancien régime* (1960), translated into English as *Centuries of Childhood: A Social History of Family Life* (1962). Ariès controversially argued that 'in medieval society, the idea of childhood did not exist'. Professional historians, notably Geoffrey Elton, were dismissive, but this opprobrium merely spurred Ariès on. His style is opinionated, discursive, speculative and polemical, which enraged the academy, and which makes him worth reading.

Ariès spent fifteen years gathering material for his monumental history of death and dying, *L'Homme devant la mort* (1977), translated into English as *The Hour of our Death* (1981). The book is a richly detailed account of death, funeral practices and mourning rituals in Western Europe during the last millennium. It is a long book, in parts quite dull, stuffed with detail on such arcane topics as French probate laws in the seventeenth century. Ariès described how death in pre-industrial Europe was distinguished by acceptance and a lack of evasion. He called this 'tame death'. Communality and openness gave death its 'tamed' quality. Tame death was characterized by 'indifference, resignation, familiarity, and lack of privacy'. The interval from the onset of illness to death was usually short. Ariès quotes from the biography of the priest and writer, Guillaume Pouget, in which he describes the death of his mother, an elderly French peasant woman:

> In [18]'74, she contracted a summer cholera. After four days she asked to see the village priest, who came and wanted to give her the last rites. 'Not yet, M. le curé, I'll let you know when the time comes.' Two days later: 'Go and tell M. le curé to bring me Extreme Unction.'

This was a typical 'tame death': swift, accepted, familiar – the priest more important than the doctor. Most importantly, everyone – from the dying woman to the priest – knew and understood their role. Ariès identified the historical and social forces which led to death becoming 'hidden': industrialization and the consequent flight from the country to the city; the decline in religious belief, which began with the Enlightenment; the development of scientific medicine; the rise of the hospital; and the establishment of the funeral industry:

> For until now, incredible as it may seem, human beings as we are able to perceive them in the pages of history have never really known the fear of death. Of course they were afraid to die; they felt sad about it, and they said so calmly. But this is precisely the point: their

anxiety never crossed the threshold into the unspeakable, the inexpressible. It was translated into soothing words and channelled into familiar rites. People paid attention to death. Death was a serious matter, not to be taken lightly, a dramatic moment in life, grave and formidable, but not so formidable that they were tempted to push it out of sight, run away from it, act as if it did not exist, or falsify its appearances.

When it was tame, 'death was not a personal drama but an ordeal for the community'. The community tamed death by ritual:

> The ritualization of death is a special aspect of the total strategy of man against nature, a strategy of prohibitions and concessions. This is why death has not been allowed its natural extravagance but has been imprisoned in ceremony, transformed into spectacle. This is also why it could not be a solitary adventure but had to be a public phenomenon involving the whole community.

Ariès conceded, however, that ritual could go only so far in taming death: 'Death may be tamed, divested of the blind violence of natural forces, and ritualized, but it is never experienced as a natural phenomenon. It always remains a misfortune, a *mal-heur*.'

Ariès showed how ritual dominated pre-industrial culture, and guided people through life's crises: 'Once, there were codes for all occasions, codes for revealing to others feelings that were generally unexpressed, codes for courting, for giving birth, for dying, for consoling the bereaved. These codes no longer exist. They disappeared in the late nineteenth and twentieth centuries.' The codes were largely governed by organized religion: books about the art of dying – the *ars moriendi* – were popular in the Middle Ages and provided spiritual instruction on how to prepare for death. When we ceased to believe (or at any rate, to worship) we found ourselves rudderless, unsure about the ritual, without a script.

Our ancestors regarded death as a process of transfer to another life. The people who lived in medieval Europe seem to have truly believed not only in heaven and hell, but also in such entities as purgatory and even limbo (abolished by papal decree in 2007). The Christian faithful went to extraordinary lengths to limit their time in purgatory, by buying plenary indulgences, going on pilgrimages, and in the case of the very wealthy, by endowing churches and monasteries.

Ariès paints a bleak picture of death in the late twentieth century: 'It [death] has now been so obliterated from our culture that it is hard for us to imagine or understand it. The ancient attitude in which death is close and familiar yet diminished and desensitized is too different from our own view, in which it is so terrifying that we no longer dare say its name.'

Society and families, he believed, had abdicated their responsibility to the dying man, passing 'this responsibility on to the scientific miracle worker, who possessed the secrets of health and sickness and who knew better than anyone else what should be done'. But the 'scientific miracle worker' was ill-equipped to deal with the reality of dying. Ariès wondered how traditional rituals about mourning all but disappeared in the twentieth century: '...the community feels less and less involved in the death of one of its members... The community in the traditional sense of the word no longer exists. It has been replaced by an enormous mass of atomized individuals.'

Although Ariès acknowledged the benign influence of the hospice movement, and the work of Elisabeth Kübler-Ross and others, he did not believe that death would ever be 're-tamed'. Ariès wrote his book in the mid-1970s, when the hospice movement was in its infancy, and he predicted that hospices would take over what should rightfully be the duties of the family and community. Neither did he approve of the syringe-driver, which robbed the dying person of his moment of leave-taking: '...the patient's passivity is maintained by sedatives, especially at the end...'

Ariès was a romantic reactionary who looked back to an idealized, pre-industrial past where life was governed by community, family and religion. He lamented the individualism, egoism and atomization of modern Europe. He correctly argued for the importance of community and ritual. But I am not persuaded that death in Ariès's Middle Ages was as painless and easy as he seems to suggest. The death of the 16th century French philosopher Montaigne (see Chapter 8) was, I suspect, typical of 'tame death': public, acknowledged and ritualized, certainly, but also full of pain, terror and horror.

GEOFFREY GORER:
THE PORNOGRAPHY OF DEATH

The British anthropologist Geoffrey Gorer (1905–85) was, like Philippe Ariès, a scholar who worked outside the academy. His inherited wealth gave him the freedom and luxury to indulge his passions. After a brilliant undergraduate career at Jesus College, Cambridge, where he graduated with a double-first in classics and modern languages in 1927, he embarked on an abortive career as a playwright and novelist. He then wrote a well-received critical study, *The Revolutionary Ideas of the Marquis de Sade* (1934), which, among other things, attempted to explain popular support for the Nazis in psychological, rather than political, terms.

In 1934, with the insouciance typical of his class and social milieu, Gorer took his male lover, the Senegalese ballet dancer Ferál Benga, to the French colonies of West Africa. They travelled from Dakar through Senegal, Guinea, the Ivory Coast, Dahomey and Nigeria. *Africa Dances*, his account of this journey, was a bestseller, and brought Gorer to the attention of the anthropologist Margaret Mead. Mead, along with her lover and colleague Ruth Benedict, instructed Gorer in social anthropology. He had found his calling: Gorer studied and wrote about not only 'primitive' peoples, such as the Himalayan Lepchas, but also about developed societies, such as Japan, the US and his native Britain.

His writing style is limpid, authoritative, untainted by jargon. Gorer was also a literary critic, who numbered W. H. Auden and George Orwell among his friends. His closest friend, however, was Margaret Mead, with whom he maintained an intense correspondence and holidayed with annually. Many speculated that they might marry, but this was never likely since, although Mead was bisexual, Gorer was exclusively gay.

Gorer wrote a famous essay, 'The Pornography of Death', published in *Encounter* in 1955, in which he argued that death had replaced sex as the great contemporary taboo: 'The natural processes of corruption and decay have become disgusting, as disgusting as the natural processes of birth and copulation were a century ago.'

Gorer, anticipating Ariès, described a pre-industrial world where

> ...funerals were the occasion of the greatest display for working class, middle class, and aristocrat. The cemetery was the centre of every old-established village, and they were prominent in most towns ... In the 20th century, however, there seems to have been an unremarked shift in prudery; whereas copulation has become more and more 'mentionable', particularly in the Anglo-Saxon societies, death has become more and more 'unmentionable' *as a natural process...*

Gorer linked this change in attitudes to death with the decline in religious belief:

> But in England, at any rate, belief in the future life as taught in Christian doctrine is very uncommon today even in the minority who make church-going or prayer a consistent part of their lives; and without some such belief natural death and physical decomposition have become too horrible to contemplate or discuss.

In 1961, Gorer's brother Peter died of cancer, leaving a wife and children. He was only fifty-four and an eminent immunologist whose work eventually made human organ transplantation possible. Peter Gorer was a Fellow of the Royal Society and, had he survived, he would have almost certainly won the Nobel Prize for Medicine. A heavy smoker, he died quickly after he was diagnosed with lung cancer. Geoffrey Gorer took charge of the burial and looked after his sister-in-law, niece and nephew. He was struck by the rejection of traditional ways of behaving, and by the harmful effects of this rejection on the bereaved. The experience inspired him to write *Death, Grief, and Mourning in Contemporary Britain* (1965). The book was based on a survey of 1,628 people, undertaken in May 1963.

Gorer described how his friends were offended by his decision to go into formal mourning after the death of his brother: 'A couple of times I refused invitations to cocktail parties, explaining that I was in mourning; the people who invited me responded to this statement with shocked embarrassment, as if I had voiced some appalling obscenity.' He speculated that the origins of this attitude date back to the Great War, when the numbers of casualties were so overwhelming that the only way of dealing with it was to grieve communally, but to remain stoical about one's personal loss. Another commentator, Pat Jalland, referred to this as 'the suppression of privatised grieving'. Gorer observed, too, that society tacitly demanded that the bereaved keep their grief to themselves. In Britain and the US, the trend was 'to treat mourning as morbid self-indulgence, and to give social admiration to the bereaved who hide their grief so fully that no one would guess anything had happened'.

Gorer concluded that, compared to their grand-parents, '...the majority of British people are today without adequate guidance as to how to treat death and bereavement and without social help in living through and coming to terms with the grief and mourning which are the inevitable responses in human beings to the death of someone they have loved.' 'The Pornography of Death' concluded with a plea: '...then we must give back to death – natural death – its parade and publicity, re-admit grief and mourning'.

ERNEST BECKER:
THE DENIAL OF DEATH

The death taboo reached its zenith (or nadir) in the US in the late twentieth century. Perhaps America, which had conquered the world, subconsciously believed that it could conquer death too. Richard Nixon famously declared 'War on Cancer' in 1971. Three years later, Ernest Becker (1924–74), an obscure cultural anthropologist, won the Pulitzer Prize posthumously for his 1973 book *The Denial of Death*. It is difficult to believe that it was widely read, since the prose is in places impenetrable, his argument conveyed through the prism of classical psychoanalytical theory ('the meaning of anality') and heavily influenced by the work of Otto Rank, a disciple of Freud's. In Woody Allen's *Annie Hall* (1977), Allen's character, the death-phobic, psychoanalysis-obsessed Alvy Singer, gives Annie (Diane Keaton) a copy of *The Denial of Death*.

The book, however, has a certain potency because Becker was dying from cancer when he wrote it, and succumbed in 1974, aged forty-nine. If Freud taught that sex was the basic motivation for human behaviour, Becker argued instead that it is our fear of death:

> ...the idea of death, the fear of it, haunts the human animal like nothing else; it is the mainspring of human activity – activity designed largely to avoid the fatality of death, to overcome it by denying in some way that it is the final destiny for man... This is the terror: to have emerged from nothing, to have a name, consciousness of self, deep inner feelings, an excruciating inner yearning for life and self-expression – and with all this yet to die.

Becker, like his contemporary Philippe Ariès, thought that the Enlightenment and scientific 'progress' had come with a heavy price-tag:

The man of knowledge in our time is bowed down under a burden he never imagined he would ever have: the overproduction of truth that cannot be consumed. For centuries man lived in the belief that truth was slim and elusive and that once he found it the troubles of mankind would be over. And here we are in the closing decades of the 20th century, choking on truth...

Becker went a step further than Ariès and Gorer, and argued that we sublimate our fear of extinction into what he called 'heroic projects', designed to transcend death. These projects included organized religion and the great political movements of the twentieth century, communism and fascism. The philosopher Sam Keen, in the Foreword to a new edition of *The Denial of Death*, wrote that Becker had discovered 'a science of evil'. Keen summarized Becker's ideas:

The first strand. The world is terrifying... The second strand. The basic motivation for human behaviour is our biological need to control our basic anxiety, to deny the terror of death... The third strand. Since the terror of death is so overwhelming we conspire to keep it unconscious... The fourth strand. Our heroic projects that are aimed at destroying evil have the paradoxical effect of bringing more evil into the world.

It is not difficult to see how Woody Allen/Alvy Singer would be attracted to Becker's pessimism: 'Creation is a nightmare spectacular taking place on a planet that has been soaked for hundreds of millions of years in the blood of all its creatures.'

The contemporary writer and philosopher John Gray, whose work is also characterized by a bracing pessimism, has clearly been influenced by Becker: 'Those who struggle to change the world see themselves as noble, even tragic figures,' Gray writes, 'Yet most of those who work for world betterment are not rebels against the scheme of things. They seek consolation for a truth they are too weak to bear. At bottom, their faith that the world can be transformed by human will is a denial of their own mortality.'

Becker's work inspired a whole new school of experimental psychology called terror management theory (TMT). TMT argues that the clash of our desire to live with our awareness of the inevitability of death creates the potential for terror. Tom Pyszczynski, one of the founders of TMT, wrote: 'Cultural worldviews manage existential terror by providing a meaningful, orderly, and comforting conception of the world that helps us come to grips with the problem of death.' Pyszczynski and others have carried out a series of controlled experiments which show that when people are given reminders of their mortality, they are more likely to be critical of, and punitive towards, those who oppose their beliefs.

TMT enthusiasts saw 9/11 as a vast natural experiment designed to test this theory. They concluded that Americans behaved in the aftermath of this disaster exactly as TMT would have predicted, with increased nationalism, intolerance of dissent, hostility towards those who are different, desire for revenge, a need for heroes, a desire to help.

Flight from Death: The Quest for Immortality, a documentary film based on the ideas of Ernest Becker and TMT, was an unlikely international success in 2003. Perhaps it is not so surprising; TMT is a sort of Grand Unified Theory of human behaviour and evil.

IVAN ILLICH:
MEDICALIZING DEATH

'Doctors are the new mediums, the decoders of the psychological mysteries of their time,' wrote Philippe Ariès, but it could just as easily have been written by Ivan Illich. Illich (1926–2002) was a singular figure. Born in Vienna to a Croatian Catholic father and a German Jewish mother, he spoke over a dozen languages fluently and often remarked that he had no mother tongue. His family had to leave Vienna after the Anschluss in 1938. Illich initially studied science (histology and crystallography), but switched to philosophy, history and theology, taking a doctorate in History at Salzburg, and studied for the priesthood at the Gregorian University in Rome. He was ordained a priest in 1950 and moved to New York, where he ministered to the Puerto Rican community. In 1956, aged just thirty, he was appointed vice-rector of the Catholic University in Ponce, Puerto Rico. Illich became a radical 'anti-imperialist' and his anti-American views led to clashes with the Catholic hierarchy, which culminated in a recall to New York in 1960.

In 1961, with the support of the American Catholic hierarchy, he established a centre in Cuernavaca in Mexico called the Center for Intercultural Formation, or Centro Intercultural de Formación (CIF). The purpose of this centre was to prepare North American missionaries for work in Latin America and to provide intensive courses in Spanish. Illich began to question the entire missionary enterprise in South America and effectively sabotaged the programme by openly discouraging would-be missionaries and writing incendiary articles attacking the American mission. CIF evolved into CIDOC (Centro Intercultural de Documentación), a sort of informal university and radical think tank. In 1968, Illich was called to the Vatican to answer charges of heresy; although no formal charges were made, he resigned from the public duties of the priesthood. Nevertheless, he continued to regard himself as a priest for the rest of his life.

It is difficult to categorize Illich: he was a medieval historian, a social theorist, a philosopher, a theologian and an educationalist. His core thesis, which he developed at CIDOC, and which has a whiff of Rousseau, was that industrialization and urbanization had robbed people in developed countries of their freedom and their spirituality. One of his best-known works, *Medical Nemesis* (1975) opens with the famous assertion: 'The medical establishment has become a major threat to health.' In this radical polemic, Illich argued that modern medicine had hubristically taken on a mission to eradicate pain, sickness, and even death. These were, he argued, eternal human realities, with which we must learn to cope: in fact, coping with these verities is what it means to be 'healthy'. Although I don't think Illich coined the word 'iatrogenesis' – meaning the harm done by doctors – he certainly popularized it. He described three types of iatrogenesis: clinical, or the direct harm done by various medical treatments; social, or the medicalization of ordinary life; and cultural, the loss of traditional ways of dealing with suffering: medicine 'constitutes a prolific bureaucratic program based on the denial of each man's need to deal with pain, sickness and death'. This medicalization of death, he argued, caused us to lose our ability to accept death and suffering as aspects of life, and to devalue our traditional rituals around death and dying. He went further: medicalization is a form of social control, in which a rejection of 'patienthood' is viewed as a form of deviance.

Illich's prose is dense and difficult; his use of footnotes is greater even than the late David Foster Wallace. His scholarship, however, is unarguable. Illich's arguments were not taken seriously enough at the time because he overstated his case, and proposed no practical solutions. The medical establishment dismissed him as a crank and moved on. Illich himself became an increasingly marginal figure. Although disowned by the church, he held visiting professorships in several European universities, after closing CIDOC in 1976. Illich himself had something of the ancient Greek philosopher Diogenes about him: he never wore a watch, which he called a 'gauge', and which he believed forced an artificial structure on daily life, yet he frequently asked the time from 'gauge bearers'. He spent most of his later life living in a mud hut just outside Mexico City, 'aristocratically aloof, austere, absorbed but happy', according to his obituary *in The Times*. There was more than a touch of the Old Testament prophet in Illich's public persona; indeed, he was frequently dismissed by critics in ad hominem attacks as a 'Jeremiah'.

It is tempting to dismiss Illich as just another historical footnote to the counter-culture of the 1960s and 1970s, and yet, nearly forty years on, much of what he warned against has come to pass. Since the publication of *Medical

Nemesis, US spending on health care as a percentage of GDP has doubled. Illich would have been wryly amused by the invention of new diseases, such as social anxiety disorder (shyness), male-pattern alopecia (baldness) and erectile dysfunction (impotence), all of which can now be medicated. The ever-increasing venality of the pharmaceutical industry would not have surprised him. How he would have loved to attack the sacred cow that is 'evidence-based medicine'. Illich wrote: 'Through the medicalization of death, health care has become a monolithic world religion... the struggle against death, which dominates the life-style of the rich, is translated by development agencies into a set of rules by which the poor of the earth shall be forced to conduct themselves.'

Illich believed that there is a profound difference between pain and suffering. Pain, he argued, is a sensation, but suffering is a practice. Pain could be borne with dignity by 'duty, love, fascination, routines, prayer and compassion'. Cultural iatrogenesis has robbed people in Western countries of their ability to suffer. Medicine, which convinced people that all pain is curable, has made pain unendurable. He predicted that this medicalization might eventually lead to assisted suicide being seen as a human right: 'The patient's unwillingness to die on his own makes him pathetically dependent. He has now lost faith in his ability to die, the terminal shape that health can take, and has made the right to be professionally killed into a major issue.'

'Dying', wrote Illich, 'has become the ultimate form of consumer resistance.'

Ivan Illich, in his fifties, developed a facial cancer, for which he typically refused treatment, or even investigation; he believed in 'the liberty to die without a diagnosis'. The cancer slowly advanced, causing considerable pain and disfigurement, and eventually killed him in 2002 at the age of seventy-six. His obituary reported:

> As the tumour on his cheek became more promi-
> nent and painful and subject to epileptic attacks, he
> refused to accept the diagnosis imposed by the doc-
> tors. 'I am not ill, it's not an illness', he declared. 'It
> is something completely different – a very compli-
> cated relationship.'

All four of these thanatologists are dead now. Ariès died aged sixty-nine; I hope his funeral was traditionally conducted and well attended, and that his family observed a suitable period of mourning. Gorer lived to eighty, and died in his manor house in Sussex, where he had cultivated his prize-winning rhododendrons. His closest friends – Orwell, Auden and Mead – predeceased him. I trust his relatives went into formal mourning.

RITUAL AND MOURNING

The bleakest funeral I ever attended was that of my friend, S. He died in Amsterdam in 2000, at the age of only forty-seven. He had lived in Holland for many years, where he worked in construction, and had married a Dutch woman, with whom he had two teenage children. He had become unwell, complaining of pains in his left arm and shoulder. Although he was a smoker with a strong family history of heart disease, his doctor thought these pains were muscular. He died suddenly of a heart attack. I travelled from Leeds (where I was living at the time) to Amsterdam for the funeral. My friend had emigrated from his native west Cork more than twenty-five years before, and left behind all those things about Ireland that he regarded as backward, such as religion. His funeral, therefore, was a singularly secular event.

I got a taxi from the airport to a huge cemetery in the suburbs of Amsterdam, and met my friend's three brothers at the entrance. They greeted me ruefully and thanked me for travelling. His widowed mother did not travel; the furthest she had ever ventured from their small farm was to the city of Cork. A business-like undertaker took control of the proceedings, and we followed him and the coffin – no 'open coffin' here – in the rain to the recently dug grave. The coffin was lowered into the ground and we few mourners simply walked away – without prayers or words of any kind. We gathered in a public room attached to the cemetery and were given coffee. The undertaker asked in a desultory fashion if anyone wanted to say a few words. The three brothers looked at each other and shook their heads: this was a task for a priest. But there was no priest, only the brusque Dutch funeral director. After a long and painful silence, one of my friend's Dutch workmates stepped shyly forward and gave a short speech – mainly in Dutch – concluding 'he was a good guy'. A CD of some folk songs that the dead man had loved was played. And that was it.

I got a taxi back to Schiphol airport where I had several hours to think about the importance of ritual in dealing with death. My friend's three brothers, reared in the Catholic tradition, were literally dumbstruck by this secular event: the banality of it was heart-breaking.

Years later, I was deeply impressed by how Catholic ritual – after the deaths of my uncle (March 2013) and father-in-law (October 2013) – guided the bereaved during the days immediately following their deaths. Ritual helps the dying too: in Ireland, the sacrament of anointing the sick carries a powerful significance even for those with little or no religious belief. This is not something a lay hospital chaplain can do. Karen Armstrong, the historian of religion, has argued that religion is about practice, rather than belief; about doing, not dogma. Our ancestors had a communal

knowledge of how to mourn, and ritual was at the core
of this knowledge.

Alain de Botton has suggested in *Religion for Atheists*
that we should cherry-pick some of the good ideas
from organized religion and adapt them for our bright,
modern secular world, while ditching what he sees as
all the superstitious, supernatural nonsense: 'Many of
the problems of the modern soul can successfully be
addressed by solutions put forward by religion, once these
solutions have been dislodged from the supernatural
structure within which they were first conceived.' De
Botton lists many of the positive aspects of organized
religion, such as the way it brings people together as a
community, the weekly opportunity to simply sit and
engage in contemplation, and the comforting rituals
around birth, marriage and death.

His case is well argued, but it seems to me that religion
has developed and refined these rituals over millennia, so
why bother inventing new ones? Why build new Temples
to 'Perspective' and 'Reflection' when we already have
the great cathedrals, temples and mosques? De Botton
describes one such doomed attempt to invent a godless
religion, namely the French philosopher Auguste Comte's
'religion for humanity'. I wonder if we should simply
be content with belonging, and stop being so worried
about believing. Evangelical atheism has accelerated the
flight from religion, leaving us even more adrift, more

atomized, and unsure of how to behave when faced with the great events of our lives.

So we have to fashion our own *ars moriendi*. It has been said that death hasn't quite come out of the closet, but its toe is sticking out. Any priest will tell you that funerals have become increasingly informal, and are now more representative of the individual than the community. Up until very recently, traditional Irish Catholics thought it vulgar to talk about the deceased, personally and specifically, from the altar during the funeral mass; now, the eulogy has become a central part of the occasion. Coffins are commonly draped with mementos such as mobile phones and replica sports jerseys. The deceased is celebrated as a wacky individualist. In crematoria, the coffin often disappears to the tune of 'My Way' or 'Always look on the bright side of life'. Ariès's 'tame death' may have been 'tame' in the sense that it was acknowledged and accepted, but it was still awesome, terrible and grand. Now, we strive to make death tame again by a kind of studied frivolousness.

I lived in Britain for fourteen years. My wife is Scottish, and my two children were born in Yorkshire. Coming from Ireland and a Catholic upbringing, I found British mourning practices very alien. An English colleague of mine died relatively young – in her early sixties – from cancer. A mutual friend, a senior doctor at the hospital, had been closely associated professionally with the dead woman for more than two decades. I was surprised, therefore, not to see him at the funeral service. I mentioned this a few days later to him, and he told me that unfortunately the funeral had coincided with a professional meeting which he was unable to reschedule. In Ireland, this would have been unthinkable. I was similarly surprised when, after the death of my father-in-law, his next-door neighbours called to the house to commiserate. We invited them in and gave them tea. When asked if they would like to see the dead man, they recoiled, saying they would like to remember him as he was.

The Irish, for all our many failings, still – just – do mourning well. The old ritualistic Catholic sequence – first the rosary, then the removal, and finally the funeral mass and burial, still survives. Rural folk still hold a 'month's mind' mass, a month after the death. The formulaic words – 'sorry for your trouble' – are still intact. Since returning to Ireland in 2001, I have been to countless removals. Funeral-going in Ireland can be excessive: I have felt obliged to attend the removals or funerals of people I have never even met – usually the parents and relatives of work colleagues. The queues are sometimes so long that it can take more than an hour to reach the top: queue-jumping at removals is a regular sight.

One of my great-uncles was a notably enthusiastic funeral-goer. Irish funerals are famously sociable events, with much food and drink provided; if the deceased is very old, the atmosphere is light-hearted, almost celebratory. In his retirement, this great-uncle travelled all over County Cork and beyond, to attend the funerals of persons with whom he often had only the most tangential and remote connection. The death notices of the *Cork Examiner* constituted his only reading material. Had he survived into the age of the Internet, he would have been an avid user of the website RIP.ie.

In the cities, however, these rituals and codes are slowly dying; in the space of a single generation, Ireland has gone from a country with near-universal church attendance to a secular society in which weekly worship is now a minority activity.

One of the few books I inherited from my father was *Irish Wake Amusements* by Seán Ó Súilleabháin. This slim volume, originally written in Irish as *Caitheamh Aimsire ar Thórraimh*, is a scholarly account of wake customs in rural Ireland in the eighteenth and nineteenth centuries, with detailed descriptions of the rituals, games and drinking which occurred at these events:

> Storytelling; singing; music and dancing; card-playing; riddles, tongue-twisters; versifying and rep-etition of Jingles... Contests in strength, agility, dexterity, accuracy of aim, endurance and tough-ness, hardihood and athletics... Taunting and

mocking, booby traps, mischief-making, horse-
play, rough games, fights... imitative games, catch
games, games of hide, seek and guessing.

When this book was first published in 1961, the author
(correctly) assumed the religious beliefs of his readership:

As Christians, it is difficult for us to imagine how
people in pagan times regarded Death and what
might follow it. They knew by experience that Death
ended the normal way of life which the deceased
had known. Still, they believed that, in some way or
another, 'life' of some kind continued beyond the
grave. Christianity taught them gradually about the
existence of the human soul which was not ended by
Death; nevertheless, they felt that the dead were still
involved in some way in human affairs, still continuing in some kind of human form which was rather
like that held during life.

Ó Súilleabháin here writes about 'the existence of the
human soul' as if its discovery was a scientific fact,
akin to a sub-atomic particle. He viewed these wake
practices as 'pagan' in origin, and 'certain aspects of
traditional wakes' were eventually stamped out by the
clergy, using pulpit denunciation and various synodal
decrees. 'Certain aspects of traditional wakes' or 'wake

abuses' almost certainly involved sex and alcohol, but Ó Súilleabháin could not go into any great detail about this when he wrote his book. Nor could he have foreseen how Ireland would shortly and dramatically shed its Christianity.

Wakes are now rare, even in Ireland, and tame events compared to the Dionysian extravaganzas described in *Irish Wake Amusements*. The last wake I attended was that of an old neighbour, the wife of the man from our street who had dropped dead at forty. She had more than forty years of widowhood, and had died a great-grandmother. It was held in the little house where she had raised her six children and she was laid out in the front parlour – the 'good room'; neighbours arrived in a regular stream and remarked how beautiful she looked. I sat next to the open coffin, and had tea and cake with her family. It was a happy, creaturely gathering and there was something about it that was intimate and serene – the fine old woman, the modest room. That which caused revulsion in Dumfries, in Cork was companionable and easy.

My aunt, a nun in the Bon Secours order, died in 2010 after many years of severe dementia. During these years, she had been cared for in the convent infirmary with a love and attentiveness that was the most persuasive argument for Christianity that I have encountered. When she died, her fellow sisters gathered in the small sitting-room of the nuns' infirmary, where she was laid out. After the recitation of the rosary, they sang hymns; the sound of these old women's voices had a strange grandeur and pathos.

Death has become fashionable as a topic of public discussion, but, despite all the celebrity memoirs and earnest newspaper articles, it is still largely hidden. In Europe, the process of secularization has advanced so far that we will never see a return to Philippe Ariès's 'tame death'. Could we fashion a secular version of tame death? I doubt it: death is tamed by ritual, and ritual is primarily a religious phenomenon. We will never go back to a pre-Enlightenment Christianity in Europe, and secular rituals will not emerge.

Perhaps it is impossible for us, afflicted by a lethal combination of secularism and individualism, to see inside the minds of our ancestors. In our atomized world, death is far more shocking for us because we cannot imagine anything beyond this self, this life.

CHAPTER 3

A Hesitation to be Brave

When Philippe Ariès described how 'tame death' gradually became 'hidden death', he called it 'the beginning of the lie', and used Tolstoy's novella *The Death of Ivan Ilyich* (1886) as a key text to illustrate this dramatic shift in human behaviour. Ilyich is a successful judge in his forties. His life is devoted to advancing his career and maintaining the proprieties of his bourgeois life. He has grown distant from his vain, superficial wife, and concerns himself with house furnishings and card-games. He is taken ill with a vague pain in his abdomen, which is diagnosed by various doctors as 'appendicitis' and a 'loose kidney'. His pain gradually gets worse, and it

eventually becomes clear that he is dying. His family and
the doctors try to hide the awful truth from him:

> Ivan Ilyich's great misery was due to the deception
> that for some reason or other everyone kept up with
> him – that he was simply ill, and not dying, and that
> he need only keep quiet and follow the doctor's
> orders, and then some great change for the better
> would be the result. He knew that whatever they
> might do, there would be no result except more
> agonizing sufferings and death. And he was made
> miserable by this lie, made miserable at their refusing
> to acknowledge what they all knew and he knew, by
> their persisting in lying over him about his awful
> position, and in forcing him too to take part in this
> lie. Lying, lying, this lying carried on over him on the
> eve of his death, and destined to bring that terrible
> solemn act of his death down to the level of all their
> visits, curtains, sturgeons for dinner... was a horrible
> agony for Ivan Ilyich. And, strange to say, many times
> when they had been going through the regular
> performance over him, he had been within a hair's
> breadth of screaming at them: 'Cease your lying! You
> know, and I know, that I'm dying; so do, at least, give
> over lying!' But he never had the spirit to do this. The
> terrible, awful act of his dying was, he saw, by all those
> about him, brought down to the level of a casual,

unpleasant, and to some extent indecorous, incident (somewhat as they would behave with a person who should enter a drawing-room smelling unpleasant). It was brought down to this level by that very decorum to which he had been enslaved all his life.

Towards the end, Ilyich realizes that he had 'not lived as one ought', that his death, like his life, was full of lies. 'From that moment', writes Tolstoy, 'there began the scream that never ceased for three days, and was so awful that through two closed doors one could not hear it without horror.' Only at the very end does Ilyich experience any peace, when his young son takes his hand, and the dying man feels tenderness and forgiveness for his family.

Ivan Ilyich's agony is an example of what Cicely Saunders, the founder of the hospice movement in Britain, called 'total pain'. By this she meant a kind of suffering beyond physical pain, marked by hopelessness, loneliness and existential despair. In my view, *The Death of Ivan Ilyich* is the most powerful, the most true, depiction of dying in fiction. The novella has had a strange afterlife: *ivans xtc.* (2002), a film loosely based on the story, is an account of the final days of an amoral Hollywood agent who is dying of cancer. Nowadays, 'the scream that never ceased for three days' would have been drowned out by the syringe-driver, but The Lie is alive and well.

In 1923, Dr Felix Deutsch examined his patient, the sixty-seven-year-old Sigmund Freud, and found that he had an oral cancer. Deutsch confided in six of Freud's closest associates, and it was decided that the great man must not be told. Later, when Ernest Jones – psychoanalyst and author of the first major biography of Freud – admitted to Freud that the truth had been kept from him, he demanded, '*Mit welchem Recht?*' ('With what right?'). Deutsch resigned as Freud's personal physician and was replaced by a young doctor called Max Schur. At their first meeting, Freud told Schur what he considered the two most important elements of the doctor–patient relationship: first, that they always tell each other the truth, and second, 'that when the time comes, you won't let me suffer unnecessarily'.

John McGahern wrote about his mother's death in *Memoir*. (McGahern himself was sickening when he wrote this book, and mortally ill by the time of publication.) She had been diagnosed with breast cancer during pregnancy, and went to the Mater Hospital in Dublin for treatment: 'When we asked about her we were warned not to ask but to pray to God. To veil everything in secrecy and darkness was natural to my father, and it turned out that my mother was far from happy with this secrecy.'

Meanwhile her husband, McGahern's monstrous police sergeant father, was secretly corresponding with his wife's surgeon: 'Dear Sir,... Would you, therefore be good enough to advise me on the following: 1. Should my wife give up teaching? 2. What is your opinion of her chances of recovery? 3. What roughly are the percentages of recovery from her disease taken at this stage she was operated on?'

The surgeon duly replied: 'She probably has a 30% chance of complete recovery.' Clearly, patient confidentiality was not greatly observed in 1940s Ireland. McGahern observed: 'He communicated neither this nor the previous report to my mother or to anybody else...' McGahern's mother died, attended only by her sister and a nurse. Her husband was stationed in the police barracks of another town. The children were taken away before the end to the barracks and their father, and his world of secrecy and evasion. His mother's death was 'hidden':

Those who are dying are marked not only by themselves but by the world they are losing. They have become the other people who die and threaten the illusion of endless continuity. Life goes on, but not for the dying, and this must be hidden or obscured or denied... My mother's faith must have been a strength, but even this was used against her when my father accused her of losing her faith in God. No matter how strong that faith was, it could hardly alleviate the human pain of losing everyone

who depended on her whom she loved and held
dear. She had no one to communicate this to after
her forty-two years in a world where many loved her.

Mortality was arguably the main theme of Samuel
Beckett's work, but even he found himself powerless to
resist the Lie. In May 1954, his only brother Frank was
diagnosed with terminal lung cancer, aged fifty-two.
Beckett travelled from Paris to Dublin, where he spent
several months caring for his brother. Frank's wife and
Beckett agreed that Frank should not be told the truth, a
decision that caused Beckett great anguish, as described
by James Knowlson in *Damned to Fame*, his biography of
Beckett: 'He found that one of the worst things about
the situation was "the atmosphere of duplicity and
subterfuge", as he listened with an aching heart to his
brother making plans for better days.'

Philippe Ariès described how a key component of
the 'hidden death' was concealment of the truth from
the dying:

A new relationship had been established that brought
the dying man and his entourage closer on an
emotional level; but the initiative, if not the power,
still belonged to the dying. Here [in the 'Hidden
Death'] the relationship persists, but it has been
reversed, and the dying man has become dependent

on his entourage... When this happens – and this is the situation today – it will be assumed that it is the duty of the entourage to keep the dying man in ignorance of his condition. How many times have we heard it said of a husband, child or relative, 'At least I have the satisfaction of knowing that he never felt a thing.' 'Never feeling a thing' has replaced 'feeling his death to be imminent'.

Ariès described how 'the final dialogue' of the tame death – 'the last farewells, the last words of counsel' – had been 'abolished by the obligation to keep the dying man in ignorance'. He argued that 'The Lie' robbed the dying: 'The last communion with God and/or others was the great privilege of the dying. For centuries there was no question of depriving them of this privilege. But when the lie was maintained to the end, it eliminated this communion and its joys.'

Sherwin Nuland, the late American surgeon and writer, author of *How We Die* (1993), reflected on his experience of concealing from his dying brother the full extent of his disease. Nuland observed that the dying themselves sometimes collude in the Lie. This is usually at a subconscious level: they may not wish to face the awful truth. They may actively deny the truth. They may be afraid of 'upsetting' their relatives, or even their doctors:

At no time did I ever consider sharing with him what I knew to be the virtually certain prognosis that he would not survive till summer... Harvey Nuland had a first-class mind and two perfectly good ears, not to mention the keen degree of insight common in those accustomed to adversity, and yet – again and again – I was taken aback by the magnitude of his denial, until near his last days. There was something in him that refused the evidence of his senses. The clamor of his wish to live drowned out the pleadings of his wish to know...

Sometimes the very sick display what appears to me a remarkable indifference, a lack of curiosity. In *Nothing to be Frightened Of* (2008), his meditation on death (and his terror of it), Julian Barnes wrote about his father, who was diagnosed with cancer, which he survived: 'My father was diagnosed with Hodgkin's disease in his early fifties. He didn't ask the doctors what was wrong with him, and therefore wasn't told. He went through the treatments, and the hospital recalls, and the gradually less frequent check-ups for twenty years without ever asking.'

This is not an unusual reaction to serious illness: I have seen it many times. I suspect it is some form of primitive reflex that protects our personality from disintegrating in times of crisis. This denial, this lack of curiosity, is a recurring theme in my experience of dying. Few of us behave as we imagine we might, or hope that we would, when faced with the news that our demise is near.

'A HESITATION TO BE BRAVE'

Kieran Sweeney, a doctor and writer, was diagnosed with pulmonary mesothelioma in 2009. The condition, a type of lung cancer usually caused by exposure to asbestos, is almost invariably fatal. He wrote about his diagnosis in the *British Medical Journal*:

> The next 48 hours are spent talking to our four beautiful kids, aged mid-teens to early 20s, whose joyous careers are currently sprinkled through school, part-time jobs and university. I can't really convey in words the catastrophic hurt my news has inflicted on them, and it is an insult, which at their age they should never have to endure. I will die of this tumour, I say, and we must address that, neither accepting nor comprehending it. This tumour will kill my body, I say, but I will yield my spirit and personhood reluctantly. We embrace. They weep. I weep for them, for fear for myself, and for the unthinkable horror that they will continue to inhabit the world in which I will play no part.

These are the words of a grown-up. There is no whiff of the 'how to break bad news' workshop. No sentimentality, no aversion of the eyes from the monumental and unavoidable prospect of impending death. No foolishness about 'fighting' the cancer, or travelling to the ends of the world to find a cure. This is what 'breaking bad news' is really like. Sweeney offered practical advice to doctors caring for the dying:

> Thus I am dispatched to the kingdom of the sick permanently and irretrievably. This can never be a pleasant journey, but it can be made tolerable, dignified even. One's guides in this world have a dual role: to read the map and direct you accordingly, but also to be with you on the terrain, a place of great uncertainty. When one meets the most senior clinical staff, one is left with a sense of technical competence, undermined with some notable exceptions, by *a hesitation to be brave* [my italics]. Eye contact is avoided when one strays off the clinical map on to the metaphysical territory – I am a man devoid of hope – and circumlocution displaces a compassionate exploration of my worst fears. Perhaps, as a doctor, I present an unusually severe challenge to my fellow clinicians – I am too much like them – and the horror of what lies before me deflects clinical carers from straying onto that territory. No one can imagine the

unimaginable except those, like me, who are experiencing it.

But one's journey to this bleak place can be rendered more bearable if everyone who shares a professional role at the various staging posts bears the bleakness of the terminus in mind... In the care I have received, the transactions have been timely and technically impeccable. But the relational aspects of care lacked strong leadership and at key moments were characterized by a hesitation to be brave. What I have always feared in illness was anonymity, being packaged, losing control, not being able to say 'this is who I am'. In the end, one is left alone, here, in the kingdom of the sick.

It is telling, that in this short and powerful piece, Sweeney used the phrase 'a hesitation to be brave' twice. He died on Christmas Eve of the same year, 2009. He had been an original and eloquent commentator on medicine and its wider role. He drew attention to the limitations of evidence-based medicine, coining the term 'the information paradox' to describe the danger of information-overload distracting the doctor from his core role of relieving suffering. Here is an extract from his obituary in the *British Medical Journal*:

He later described this approach as metaphysical

and in a prescient piece he wrote, 'The clearest example of this transition to the metaphysical level occurs when someone starts to die or accepts that death is near. Here both the doctor and the patient are confronted by the question: "When is enough, enough? This", he wrote, "will be the defining question for the next generation of practitioners."'

THE DIFFICULT CONVERSATION

Enough, indeed. A word rarely used in American medicine, where the culture of medical excess is most unbridled. Atul Gawande, the American surgeon and writer, became famous for championing safe surgical surgery by adopting practices from other spheres of human activity such as the aviation industry. He writes regularly for the *New Yorker*, which published a long piece by him in 2010, called 'Letting Go: What should medicine do when it can't save your life?' This article formed the basis for his 2014 book, *Being Mortal*. He described how, in the US, dying patients are routinely subjected to futile and painful medical treatments, while their doctors fail to discuss with them the inevitable outcome: 'Patients die only once. They have no experience to draw on. They need doctors and nurses who are willing to have the hard discussions and say what they have seen, who will help people prepare for what is to come – and to escape a warehoused oblivion that few really want.'

But doctors are no longer brave enough. They increasingly see themselves as service-providers, a role that does not encourage Difficult Conversations, or a willingness to be brave. Consumerism, fear of litigation and over-regulation have conspired to create the customer-friendly doctor, who emerged when the doctor–patient relationship became recast in a quasi-commercial mould. This type of doctor, well trained in communication skills, eminently biddable, is not what Kieran Sweeney or Atul Gawande had in mind. Doctors, by the nature of their selection and training, are conformist, and the now dominant ethos of customer-friendliness has all but silenced other, dissenting, voices. There is now an insatiable appetite for medicine: for scans, for drugs, for tests, for screening. This appetite benefits many professional groups, industries and institutions. It is difficult to call 'enough', but a good doctor sometimes has to tell patients things they do not want to hear. Regrettably, it is much easier, in the middle of a busy clinic, to order another scan than to have the Difficult Conversation.

Doctors have a duty beyond that of pleasing the individual patient, a duty to society at large. The US has many so-called 'concierge' doctors, private physicians engaged by the wealthy, who are always on call to minister to the needs of their fastidious and demanding clients. The annual fee per patient is said to be as much as $30,000. The ultimate concierge doctor was Conrad Murray, the late Michael Jackson's personal physician. Murray's willingness to prescribe almost anything, including the general anaesthetic agent, propofol, for his wealthy and manipulative patient, eventually led to Jackson's death.

Axel Munthe's autobiography, *The Story of San Michele* (1929), is, in part, the story of a concierge doctor. Munthe, a Swede who had studied medicine in Paris, developed a lucrative practice, first in Paris, then in Rome, treating wealthy neurotics. Like Murray, he eventually had just one, wealthy and powerful patient, the Queen of Sweden (who was also his lover). Munthe, who had a brilliant start to his career as a medical student and young doctor, was filled with regret for the direction he had taken. Describing another concierge doctor working in Rome, Munthe wrote: 'That I considered him an able doctor was of course quite compatible with his being a charlatan – the two go well together, the chief danger of charlatans lies there.'

Patient autonomy now trumps all other rights and obligations. Autonomy, however, is a useful card to play when, as often happens, particularly with the diagnosis of cancer, I am ambushed by well-meaning relatives, urging me not to tell the patient, because 'it would kill' them.

74

Relatives have no formal rights as such, but commonly dictate medical care to those doctors keen on a quiet life and willing to be leaned on. Inevitably there will be instances, such as in the case of patients with dementia or those of very advanced age, where giving a diagnosis of cancer is of no benefit to them. But in most cases I believe it is my duty to tell the truth.

The difficulty, however, is this: Kieran Sweeney's acceptance of, and confrontation of, his situation, is the exception, not the rule. He was both advantaged and disadvantaged when he was given the diagnosis of mesothelioma. As a doctor, he knew immediately what the future held in store for him, but this knowledge precluded all hope. Many of my patients lack the educational background or knowledge to fully absorb a diagnosis of something like mesothelioma. Apart at all from this 'cognitive' aspect, many simply do not want to know the grisly details about survival statistics and what the future might hold. As the case of Sherwin Nuland's brother shows, it is not only relatives who wish to have the truth concealed. Many patients do not want to have the Difficult Conversation.

The entire modern hospital system conspires against those doctors willing to have this dialogue: the relatives, the chaos and noise of the environment, the techno-juggernaut of modern hospital care, the customer-friendly doctors who are happy and willing to dole out false, delusional hope, and sometimes the patients themselves, who may not want to hear what the doctor has to say. The temptation to opt for the quiet life, to avoid the Difficult Conversation, is overwhelming. And no one will ever complain. The relatives will be content, and the dying will soon be dead. Why give yourself the grief?

Society at large purports to want leadership and professionalism from doctors, but I wonder if this is really true. Leadership and professionalism involve confronting unpleasant truths, and sometimes denying people what they want (or think they want). Many doctors routinely over-diagnose, over-investigate and over-treat; these doctors are invariably described, approvingly, by their patients as 'thorough'. Inevitably, the 'thorough' doctors eventually leave their dying patients mystified and abandoned when there is no chemotherapy left, no scans to order.

Sherwin Nuland bitterly regretted his funking of his duty to level with his brother when he was diagnosed with advanced colon cancer: 'With this burden on my shoulders, I made a series of mistakes. That I made them with what seemed like the best of intentions does not mitigate how I feel about them in retrospect... I could not deny him a form of hope that he seemed to need.'

SENTIMENTALITY AND THE LIE

Much of the behaviour of people around the dying is characterized by sentimentality and evasion. This can take many forms: at its simplest, there are the relatives who conceal from the dying person the fact that he or she is dying. Then there are those – relatives, friends and doctors – who encourage a deluded optimism about the benefits of medical treatment. This deluded optimism is usually disguised as 'giving hope'. Friends and family may genuinely believe in the delusion, which then becomes even more difficult to deflate. Doctors generally know what is truth and what is fantasy, yet some cynically peddle lies to their patients. This may be done with the good intention of 'maintaining hope'; others become addicted to the hero-worship given by their adoring patients. Then there are the charlatans and money-grabbers – and they're not all on the fringes.

Many dying people inhabit a world of histrionic pretence. David Rieff's memoir about the death of his mother Susan Sontag, *Swimming in a Sea of Death* (2008), is a vivid depiction of such a world. Having twice survived cancer, Sontag was diagnosed with a form of bone-marrow cancer, myelodysplastic syndrome, at the age of seventy. Rieff describes his mother's terror of death, and the bizarre denial she maintained almost to the very end.

Rieff clearly knew that his mother was dying, but could not summon the courage, or find the opportunity, to discuss this with her, and the memoir is filled with regret for this failure.

The journalist John Walsh, in his memoir of his Irish immigrant parents, *The Falling Angels* (1999), expressed outrage that his doctor father, when diagnosed with leukaemia, was told that it would be fatal. Walsh describes his parents' disastrous decision to retire to their native west of Ireland, after half a lifetime in London. They found it difficult to settle, the new Ireland unrecognizable to them. Walsh's father's specialist, knowing his medical background, told him the unvarnished truth: '"You're a doctor, Martin,"' he said. "You know how these things go. Check your will, say goodbye to a few friends and accept it. That's it, I'm afraid."' Not, I'm sure, the approach they would recommend in a Breaking Bad News workshop, but I think I understand what this doctor was trying to do: speaking frankly to his patient, a colleague talking to a colleague. Walsh was appalled: 'I could never forgive the cold-hearted scumbag for saying such a thing to my poor father.'

So – there is little reward, professionally or emotionally, for doctors who tell patients the truth, but the Lie is heavily incentivized. Nearly all families, and many patients, prefer the Lie. I try to engage with the dying patient with the intention of being honest, but the path of the Lie often looks so much more inviting. And no one has ever complained to me for taking the path of the Lie. Doctors, like their patients, are human and flawed, and the easy path of the Lie is the road commonly taken.

Ivan Illich wrote scathingly of medicine's appropriation of death, but even he believed that a doctor could help the dying man: 'The old Mediterranean norm – that a wise person needs to acquire and treasure an *amicus mortis*, one who tells you the bitter truth and stays with you to the inexorable end – calls for revival. And I see no compelling reason why one who practises medicine could not also be a friend – even today.'

CHAPTER 4

How the Poor Die

The modern acute hospital, where most of us are fated to end our days, is ill equipped to meet the needs of the dying. The culture, the ambience, the tone, is of haste, bustle, frayed tempers and a strange kind of giddiness. Big teaching hospitals have too many roles: these include dealing with the acutely ill, treating major (and minor) trauma, running out-patient clinics for the chronically ill, training medical students, doctors and nurses, carrying out clinical research, treating cancer, and so on and on. Care of the dying is not a priority. A Monday morning in such a hospital has the air of a chaotic small city. The needs of patients seem to come a poor second to those of the staff and the institution. Hierarchy, professional 'turf' and protocol are paramount, with different groups competing for the finite resources, such as beds, junior staff and theatre space. Such hospitals are self-perpetuating, loosely affiliated gatherings of rival professional groups.

Medical students throng the overcrowded wards. Frail, sick, elderly people lie on trolleys, in full public view, in the main corridor of the emergency department. These pilgrims are seen and assessed by harassed, sleep-deprived, junior doctors. The doctors, from different teams and departments, sometimes argue bitterly over who is going to 'take' such patients.

Public hospitals are plagued and fettered by bogus notions of egalitarianism, which ultimately does a disservice to patients. The overwhelming impression from the various reports into the Stafford Hospital scandal in Britain was that nobody was in charge. The Francis Report on the Stafford scandal observed of the Trust board at that hospital: 'It was necessary for directors to roll up their sleeves and see for themselves what was actually happening.' There is much talk in state-funded health systems of 'clinical governance' and 'accountability', but on the wards leadership is conspicuously lacking.

The idea of 'death with dignity' in this sort of milieu is almost laughable. Peace and decorum are hard to find. Even locating a quiet room to talk to the patient and their family can be impossible; the day-room occupied by medical students, the sister's office used for the nursing handover. I have sometimes been disturbed, while at a key moment of the difficult conversation with dying patients and their families, by cleaners and porters, oblivious to the situation, intent only on completing the task at hand. Television sets and radios are set at maximum volume. Meals are often left uneaten, the patients too weak to sit up, the nurses too busy with more pressing demands to feed them.

Perhaps this lack of decorum reflects the age profile of those working there: many nurses, and most junior doctors, are young – often less than thirty. Decorum does not come naturally to the young. Young undertakers always look slightly out of place, like a bad actor in an amateur production. When I was a boy, young priests were common in Ireland. I always found them slightly absurd: being called 'Father' by old ladies, looking solemn and wise at the altar. Now I know that most of them felt anything but wise. The young too easily forget that a hospital is a place for the sick and the dying. And hospitals, no matter what American television comedy shows would have us believe, are not environments bursting with humorous possibilities. Kieran Sweeney, while dying of cancer, attacked the culture of jokiness in hospitals:

> Please can we avoid crass attempts at humour? There
> is nothing funny about clutching a plastic bag with

all your clothes in, except your pants, socks and
shoes – just stop and think what that must be like –
while trying to secure a hospital gown around you,
and following, like some faithful gun dog, a radiol-
ogy attendant who without introduction commands
you, with a broad grin to acknowledge his witty lack
of grammar, to 'follow I!'

Christmas is excruciating in this regard: for two weeks,
many hospital staff behave like five-year-olds who have
had too many fizzy drinks.

There has been an attempt in recent years to apply
hospice principles to the treatment of patients dying in
acute general hospitals, to make them 'hospice-friendly'.
In Ireland, a glossy policy document, *Quality Standards
for End-of-Life Care in Hospitals* has a foreword by former
President Mary McAleese, who writes: 'the end of life
is something deeply profound'. The programme lists
various standards, the first and most important being
'that end-of-life-care is central to the mission of the hospital and is organized around the needs of patients'.
The glossary helpfully defines death for us: 'the state or
condition of being without life, animation or activity'.
Various celebrities have supported the campaign, and
branding has been important, with a vaguely Celtic logo,
which, when displayed on the ward, indicates a recent
or impending death. The intention is that the presence

of this symbol, placed on a table outside the room, should alert staff and visitors to be quiet, to behave with decorum. 'But', said a very experienced ward sister to me, 'isn't that how you're supposed to behave *anyway*?' The programme, despite its celebrity endorsements and 'brand', has not greatly altered the quotidian realities of hospital life. 'Well-intentioned but ineffective' is the withering assessment from those on the front line. Reading this document reminded me of a priest who was a curate in my local parish when I was a boy. He had great difficulty with sermons, finding it almost impossible to conjure something original on a weekly basis. Sometimes he would become tongue-tied and couldn't think of anything to say. On these not infrequent occasions he would fill the embarrassing silence with this phrase: 'God wants ye to be as good and as kind as ye possibly can be.'

THE ROAD TO NOWHERE

The Liverpool Care Pathway (LCP) was introduced in the NHS with the best of intentions. This 'Pathway' was so-called because it was developed by palliative care physicians in that city. The idea was to apply hospice principles to the care of the dying in acute hospitals, to recognize that the process of dying had started, and to protect the patient from futile and uncomfortable medical interventions. The Pathway is, like much medical care in the NHS, guided by a detailed and proscriptive protocol, an 'algorithm', which dictates precisely what to do in any given situation. Although the Pathway did not explicitly advise the withdrawal of food and drink, there was a common perception that it did, with the inevitable accusation that the patients were being 'starved to death' or 'dying of thirst'. The Pathway simply recommended 'daily assessment of the need for clinical hydration and nutrition'. Some doctors and relatives were genuinely concerned that patients were put on the Pathway inappropriately – they weren't actually dying. Once on the Pathway, it was difficult to take a patient off it: the doctor looked vaguely ridiculous. A study found that 3 per cent of patients actually improved when they were put on the LCP. Paradoxically, this phenomenon, in some cases, could be the result of the withdrawal of intravenous fluids and nutrition in patients who, before being placed on the Pathway, had been given too much intravenous fluids and food by tube-feeding.

Nutrition has become a cause of ethical difficulty in acute hospitals. Doctors and nurses are bombarded with exhortations to screen for, and treat, malnutrition in hospital patients, particularly the elderly. All quite laudable, but very often such enthusiasm spills over into hysteria, with old, frail, sometimes dying patients subjected to tube-feeding, when a more hands-off approach is appropriate. Speech and language therapists (whose remit, as well as speech and language problems, includes difficulties with swallowing) constantly scrutinize these patients for any signs of 'unsafe swallowing', which places even greater pressure on doctors to tube-feed. The general public, not surprisingly, has become somewhat puzzled by all this: a patient might have been pressured initially into having tube-feeding, and then, if placed on the Liverpool Care Pathway, this form of nutritional support was immediately stopped. Modern hospital care seems to swing from one violent extreme to another: in a matter of days, a patient may be switched from PEG feeding to 'Nil by Mouth'. Despite all this concern about nutrition, food is often neglected. The NHS now spends more money on artificially produced 'nutritional supplements' than it does on food. Dieticians and speech and language therapists tend to focus solely on one aspect of a patient's treatment (nutrition and swallowing, respectively), and thus do not always see the bigger picture.

The doctor and broadcaster Michael O'Donnell wrote about his wife's death in the *British Medical Journal*: 'Having watched my wife, whom I loved dearly, endure attenuated "ethical" death by starvation and dehydration, I find it difficult to see the moral distinction between starving people to death and helping them end their own lives.'

I accept that the dying no longer need much in the way of food and drink, but the authors of the Pathway grievously underestimated the symbolic importance of feeding. Giving a dying man a little water or a spoonful of yoghurt achieves little from a nutritional perspective, but for the dying themselves and those attending them, it gives comfort and intimacy. A patient of mine, a man aged ninety, was approaching death after a series of acute events, including bleeding and infection. I found, to my dismay, that he had been assessed by a speech and language therapist and found to have an 'unsafe swallow', and was therefore, inevitably, put on 'nil orally'. I tried to explain, as gently as I could, to the nursing staff that the man was dying, and that any putative risk of aspiration was irrelevant. This obsession with 'unsafe swallowing' is symptomatic of the safety culture that is pervasive in acute hospitals: eliminating risk, no matter how remote, is more important than humane care, even of the dying, for whom 'risk', self-evidently, is no longer relevant.

For most dying people, however, the Pathway seems to have worked well: it completely altered the approach to their care, protecting them from futile treatment, and ensured that pain and other distressing symptoms were properly treated. Two large audits of the Pathway, however, showed that the Lie is alive and well: most patients on the Pathway did not know they were dying, and only around half knew the details of their diagnosis.

Genuine concerns about a small minority of patients inappropriately put on the Pathway were cynically seized on by the press, who accused hospitals and doctors of carrying out involuntary euthanasia, incentivized by cash bonuses. (In the target-driven NHS, hospitals were actually given bonuses for reaching specific targets on palliative care; one such target was the percentage of dying patients placed on the LCP.) Professor Mike Richards, the NHS's National Clinical Director for Cancer and End of Life Care, tried to allay public concerns: 'There is one over-arching message which the National End of Life Programme wants to emphasize to clinicians and to those with a relative who might be placed on the Pathway: the LCP has improved and continues to improve care of the patient in the last days or hours of life.'

Professor Richards's memo failed to reassure the press and the politicians, and an independent inquiry, chaired by Baroness Julia Neuberger, recommended the scrapping of the Pathway. Neuberger's report, *More Care, Less Pathway*, is commendably brief and well-written. She concluded that when the Pathway was operated by well-trained and well-resourced clinical teams, it worked well. Where care was already poor, the LCP had been used as a tick-box exercise. Neuberger observed that the word 'pathway' is misleading, as it suggests a road going somewhere. She sensibly suggested dropping the word 'pathway' in favour of the more neutral term 'end of life care plan'. Some relatives clearly believed that the Pathway represented a decision by doctors to kill their dying patients. Rather bravely, Neuberger concluded that if we don't have a proper national conversation about dying, doctors and nurses will become 'the whipping boys for an inadequate understanding of how we face our final days'.

The relatively few failures of the Pathway had fatally contaminated the 'brand' in the mind of the public. Why did it fail? Most people nowadays die after a long illness. It can be difficult, therefore, to be sure when a patient has moved from having a chronic illness to dying, or 'actively dying', as the oxymoronic term has it. Some patients were probably put on the Pathway too early; others should never have been put on the Pathway at all. The vast majority of patients, however, were put on the Pathway correctly, and had an easier death because of it.

Poor communication was at the root of virtually all complaints about the LCP. The tick-boxy forms which had to be filled in on a daily basis once the patient was placed on the Pathway gave the impression of a one-size-fits-all exercise. A palliative care physician told me: 'the Pathway looks like it was designed by a doctor with the mind of an engineer.' Before palliative care emerged as a speciality, symptom control for dying patients was haphazard and unstandardized, with many mavericks creating their own set of rules. When evidence-based palliative care emerged, it brought in an era of protocols, guidelines and audits, along with forms – lots of forms.

But dying people did benefit. The mistake was to pre-scribe for populations, not individuals.

The history of the Pathway shows the difficulties faced by doctors working in acute general hospitals. We are simultaneously accused of being too interventionist and invasive in our treatment of the dying, and too hasty in putting patients on a palliative pathway and the syringe-driver. The media – particularly the newspapers – managed to reduce a difficult and complex debate to shouty, hysterical headlines.

STAFFORD

Perhaps the greatest quantity of misinformation relating to death in acute hospitals emerged from the Stafford Hospital scandal. This episode is only one of a long line of NHS scandals dating right back to Ely Hospital in Cardiff in 1967, through to Bristol and Alder Hay Hospital in Liverpool. I worked in the NHS for fourteen years; I am, on the whole, proud to have done so. But it seems to me that the NHS, every decade or so, requires a ritual blood sacrifice. These scandals allow politicians to grandstand about patients being 'at the centre of the NHS', and after the inevitable prolonged and expensive public inquiries, and much worthy and contrite admissions of failure, it's back to business as usual.

The Stafford story unfolded slowly and innocuously. In September 2007, Julie Bailey complained about the care received by her eighty-six-year-old mother who had died at the hospital. Dissatisfied with the hospital's response, Bailey set up a local protest group called 'Cure the NHS'. Many other relatives of patients who had died at Stafford Hospital came forward, and the group met at a local café, which set up a wall with photographs of the dead. The group – and others – raised concerns about mortality rates at the hospital.

There is no doubt that care at Stafford Hospital was poor, that cruelty and neglect were common. I suspect, however, that this hospital was no better or worse than many NHS hospitals; it was probably just the dog that got a bad name. In total, there were five official investigations into care at Stafford: the first, in 2009, was carried out by the Healthcare Commission. The Department of Health commissioned two inquiries: one by the national director for acute care, and one by the national director for primary care. Sir Robert Francis, an eminent medico-legal barrister, chaired an independent inquiry, which reported in 2010. The families of patients who had died at Stafford complained that the hearings of this inquiry should have been in public. The then Labour government responded to this pressure by commissioning Francis to undertake another – public – inquiry, which sat for two and a half years, and published its final report in 2013.

The first Francis Report (2010) contains hundreds of statements from patients and relatives. Here are some of the statements which made it into the newspapers:

> 'Following a fall the patient was admitted to Stafford Hospital. When the patient requested a bedpan he was told by the nurse to soil himself as she was too busy to help…'
>
> '…his mother's bed was left soaking in urine and she developed a number of bedsores. The emergency button was often left out of reach and her son had to leave work early to ensure someone was there to help feed her.'

The press did not report the fact that there were just as many complimentary comments from patients and relatives about the hospital:

> 'On each of the six occasions when the patient attended Stafford Hospital, for hearing assessments and tests, he was dealt with in a "professional, courteous and timely manner" and has no complaints.'
>
> 'Having contracted C.difficile [a bowel infection, usually caused by antibiotics] in the community, a male patient's life was saved by two "brilliant young doctors at Stafford Hospital". He also had several skin cancers removed, his left knee replaced and

surgery on his ear. His wife had a hysterectomy and major surgery on her foot. They have always received excellent care at Stafford Hospital.'

All of these investigations concluded that care at the hospital was poor. The second Francis Report (2013) is a nuanced, detailed document, just slightly longer (at 783,710 words) than the King James Bible (783,137 words). Its conclusions, however, are predictably banal: 'What is required now is a real change in culture, a refocusing and recommitment of all who work in the NHS – from top to bottom of the system – on putting the patient first.' The report did, however, give some insight as to how care at Stafford got to be so bad. Staff numbers had been cut so the Trust could meet financial targets which would enable it to achieve Foundation Trust status; there were not enough Coronary Care, Intensive Care and High Dependency beds; relations between managers and consultants were poor. The report by the Healthcare Commission described how doctors were routinely diverted from sick patients on the wards to attending patients in the Emergency Department so that the hospital would not be in breach of a four-hour target. The politicians who expressed their shock and outrage over Stafford in parliament and in the media were often the very same politicians who had imposed this target culture on the NHS.

These accounts of unhappy experiences at Stafford Hospital bear an uncanny resemblance to George Orwell's 'How the Poor Die' (1946), an essay recounting his spell in a Paris hospital, where he was admitted with pneumonia in 1929. In Orwell's day, it was assumed that only poor people used public hospitals: 'In the public wards of a hospital you see horrors that you don't seem to meet with among people who manage to die in their own homes, as though certain diseases only attacked people at the lower income levels.' Orwell had never been in the public ward of a hospital before, and his essay describes the daily horrors of such a place: 'A hospital is a place of filth, torture and death, a sort of antechamber to the tomb.'

LIES, DAMNED LIES

Although there was an understandable public outcry over these accounts of casual cruelty and neglect, what the media and the politicians got exercised about was the concept of 'avoidable deaths'. The NHS used a statistical tool called the Hospital Standardized Mortality Ratio (HSMR) to calculate the number of expected deaths in any given hospital. This ratio is calculated by working out the risk of death associated with particular diagnoses; this risk, or ratio, is then 'adjusted', depending on the patient's age, sex, social deprivation score and type of admission (emergency or elective). Using this ratio, it was calculated that more patients died at Stafford Hospital than the NHS average.

The HSMR statistical method was developed by the Dr Foster Intelligence Unit at the School of Public Health at Imperial College London, which founded a separate campus company to exploit its commercial potential. Many questioned the statistical methodology, including Paul Taylor, an expert in health informatics, who wrote an illuminating article, 'Rigging the Death Rate' for the *London Review of Books*. (The best information and analysis of medical issues is now found, not as one would expect, in the medical journals, but in literary magazines such as the *LRB*.) Taylor and several others demonstrated the crudity of this mortality ratio. It is subject to many biases and distortions, such as the accuracy of coding, the quality of local GP care, and access to hospice care. A commercial competitor of Dr Foster Intelligence, Caspe Healthcare Knowledge Systems (CHKS), advised another hospital – Medway – which also had a high HSMR. They advised the hospital trust that it had been 'under-using' the specific code for palliative care: by increasing the proportion of patients it coded as receiving palliative care, Medway lowered its HSMR dramatically.

The first Francis Report gave a summary of an independent assessment of the HSMR statistical method by two epidemiologists from the University of Birmingham,

Professor Richard Lilford and Dr M. A. Mohammed: 'our most crucial finding is that the methodology used to derive the Dr Foster SMR is riddled with the constant risk-adjustment fallacy and so is not fit for purpose.' Even Roger Taylor, director of research at the Dr Foster Unit, lamented that the statistics had been 'woefully poorly misunderstood'. He went on: 'there is no figure for the actual number of people who might have died avoidably. It is impossible to put an actual figure on it.'

Although the public inquiries into Stafford Hospital were covered in some detail by the press, it was less widely reported that Dr Mike Laker of Newcastle University was asked by the Mid Staffordshire Trust to examine a number of cases where families felt that poor care had contributed to a relative's death. He interviewed 120 families and examined 50 case-notes, and concluded that poor care caused death in 'perhaps one'.

Even Robert Francis, in his voluminous reports, stated that no firm conclusions could be drawn from the hospital mortality figures. He acknowledged that unkindness, rather than a high death rate, was the main concern of those who had given evidence: 'It was striking how many accounts I received related to basic elements of care and the quality of the patient experience, as opposed to concerns about clinical errors leading to death or injury.' Yet the public, the media and the politicians now assume that *any* deaths above the national average must be the consequence of poor care, and thus, avoidable. The *Guardian*, in a piece by Denis Campbell headlined 'Mid Staffs hospital scandal: the essential guide', opens with the following statement: 'An estimated 400–1,200 patients died as a result of poor care over the 50 months between January 2005 and March 2009 at Stafford Hospital.' If the deaths were the result of poor care, somebody must be to blame, and there were calls for criminal prosecutions at Stafford. Peter Dominiczak in the *Daily Telegraph* reported in June 2013:

A review of deaths at Mid-Staffordshire NHS Foundation Trust by police and other officials has identified hundreds of cases between 2005 and 2009 where poor care could have led to deaths. Campaigners welcomed the announcement and warned that individuals 'must be held to account' to avoid another tragedy on a similar scale to Mid-Staffs... Politicians and campaigners have lamented the fact that no one involved in the scandal has so far faced any legal action.

So the Stafford Hospital scandal has now fixed an idea in the public consciousness of hospital death as a failure of medical care, on a par with an industrial accident, which automatically triggers an investigation by the Health and Safety Executive. This, combined with the demise of the

Liverpool Care Pathway, has, at least temporarily, put into reverse the programme of enlightened care of the dying in acute hospitals in the UK.

The various Royal Colleges felt obliged to respond to the Francis Report. The response from the Royal College of Physicians, *Putting Patients First: Realising Francis' Vision*, has the expected hand-wringing tone of such documents, with woolly aspirations about developing leadership among doctors, 'helping to improve patient experience', setting quality standards, improving training, and so on. There is a prevailing societal view that doctors and nurses must be more 'accountable' and (particularly in Britain) there are literally dozens of agencies, colleges and quangos charged with overseeing those who work in hospitals. The moral philosopher Onora O'Neill addressed this 'accountability' culture in her Reith Lectures in 2002, and observed that while in theory the new regulations make professionals more accountable, in practice they achieve little, except an increase in suspicion: 'currently fashionable methods of accountability damage rather than repair trust'.

WAREHOUSES OF THE DYING

It is a curious statistic that, in Ireland, you are three times more likely to die in an Intensive Care Unit (ICU) than in a hospice. Death in an ICU is frequently held up as an example of the worst kind of 'technological' hospital death, but is this really true? The ICU, unlike the general ward, is above all else a controlled environment. Each patient has a designated nurse looking after them, and them alone. The consultant staff are on the ground. Any acute deterioration is detected quickly and acted upon. The squalor and chaos of the general ward is not in evidence: the ambience and ethos is different. The ICU in my hospital has a 'quiet time' between 12 noon and 2 p.m., when no ward rounds or procedures take place and the lights are dimmed. About one in five patients admitted to an ICU will die there, but in most such cases, 'active' treatment has been withdrawn in the days or hours leading up to death. ICU doctors are generally anaesthetists by training, and are thus particularly good at pain relief.

So dying in an ICU may not be the worst type of hospital death. This is not the case in the US, where elderly patients with dementia and metastatic cancer are routinely admitted to an ICU. One American ICU doctor, interviewed by Atul Gawande, remarked bitterly that she was running a 'warehouse for the dying':

> Out of ten patients in her unit, she said, only two were likely to leave the hospital for any length of time. More typical was an almost eighty-year-old

woman at the end of her life, with irreversible con-
gestive heart failure, who was in the ICU for the
second time in three weeks, drugged to oblivion
and tubed in most natural orifices and a few artificial ones... Another woman, in her eighties, with
end-stage respiratory and kidney failure, had been
in the unit for two weeks. Her husband had died
after a long illness, with a feeding tube and a tracheotomy, and she had mentioned that she didn't want
to die that way. But her children wouldn't let her go,
and asked to proceed with the placement of various
devices: a permanent tracheotomy, a feeding tube,
and a dialysis catheter. So now she just lay there
tethered to her pumps, drifting in and out of
consciousness.

It has been said that in the US, only the very poor
(and thus medically uninsured) manage to die with
dignity. Intensive care is used much more sparingly in
Britain and Ireland, but the inexorable trend is towards
American-style ICU care. The average age of an ICU
patient is sixty, but many patients in their eighties and
even nineties are now admitted to ICUs, which would
not have been the case when I trained in the 1980s.
Doctors are also increasingly fearful of being labelled
as 'ageist' by relatives and also by their geriatrician
colleagues. Families, even those of the very old and frail,

are increasingly demanding maximum intervention. This is exacerbated by media scare-stories about old people being denied 'life-saving' treatments.

WILD DEATH

Most hospital deaths, however, take place, not in the ICU, but in General Medical wards, which are sometimes chaotic, understaffed and overcrowded. These wards are occupied mainly by elderly, highly dependent patients, and often there are simply not enough nurses to look after them properly. Relatives complain bitterly of their loved ones not being fed, but would rarely entertain the idea of assisting the nurses in this task, as is common in other countries. And it's a vicious circle: an overstretched nurse, lacking leadership, faced with very dependent elderly patients and complaining relatives, may quickly burn out and get through the shift doing the bare minimum. Many of the very nurses the system really needs – those with decades of ward experience – have left to pursue nine-to-five jobs as specialist and out-patient nurses, leaving the heavy lifting to the young and the inexperienced.

Patients in these general wards fall into the following three categories: first, the acutely ill; second, the 'medic-ally discharged' (previously known, uncharitably, as 'bed blockers') – old folk who have recovered from their acute illness but who cannot go home and are awaiting 'placement' in a nursing home; and third, the dying. The acutely ill patients, understandably, are the priority for the nursing and medical staff. A single acutely unstable patient commonly distracts attention from the other patients: when staff and resources are limited, these other patients may be neglected.

There are different kinds of hospital death: the rapid, acute death, caused by some sudden catastrophe such as a heart attack or a stomach haemorrhage; the semi-acute death, which occurs over weeks, from a chronic illness such as liver cirrhosis; and the slow, lingering death, such as that which eventually overtakes patients with dementia or a stroke. Ideally, patients who are acutely unstable should be treated in the Intensive Care Unit or a High Dependency Unit (a sort of halfway house between an ICU and a general ward), but beds are too few to accommodate the growing demand, so the ICU doctors can only take the very sickest.

Without exception, the worst type of hospital death is the acute death on the general ward. The patient might not be recognized initially as being sick enough to require ICU admission, or there may simply be no ICU beds. The nurse may have several other sick patients to attend to, and the first port of call for medical help is often an inexperienced and terrified intern. There is inevitably, at the end, a gruesome scene at the bedside following the unsuccessful resuscitation attempt.

Most of the deaths I witness are semi-acute or chronic. By far the commonest cause of this kind of death in my practice is from liver cirrhosis. Death in this particular group of patients is particularly difficult for people to comprehend: most of the patients are young (under fifty); the disease is 'not cancer'; there is a known 'cure' (liver transplantation). Unfortunately, most patients admitted to hospital with liver failure caused by alcoholic cirrhosis do not qualify for a transplant; you have to have demonstrated abstinence from alcohol for a minimum of six months, and (paradoxically) you have to be well enough to undergo the operation – so, for example, you have to overcome infection or kidney failure first. Liver transplantation is therefore for a very select few: if you survive the liver failure and stop drinking, you generally don't *need* one; if you go back to drinking alcohol, you don't *qualify* for it; if you're too sick, you can't *have* it. Thus liver transplantation is reserved for that minority who, despite giving up alcohol, develop recurrent liver failure, but recover sufficiently from these bouts to undergo the transplant operation. Most of my patients with alcoholic cirrhosis continue drinking, and die, sooner or later, of liver failure.

Over many years, I have become better at predicting those of my liver failure patients who will live, and those who will die. (I may be deluding myself in this regard, because several studies have shown that doctors are woefully inaccurate at predicting survival time in dying patients: they generally overestimate.) This art of prediction is a mixture of science (clinical risk scores), experience and intuition. It can be difficult, however, to persuade families that the overwhelmingly likely outcome is death. The family of the woman with liver failure I described in Chapter 1 never accepted my prognosis, a refusal which only added to the discomfort and distress of the dying woman. These patients rarely die in a hospice or at home. Most die on the acute ward, or in the ICU, after weeks, or even months, of uncomfortable and invasive treatment. Death from liver failure can be nasty and undignified, particularly if bleeding is the final insult. Luckily, most slip into a coma and are unconscious for several days before their death. I have witnessed the deaths of dozens of patients with liver cirrhosis; those who knew and understood what was happening, and who opted for a non-interventionist approach, were rare indeed.

The family of one patient of mine did however take my advice, and gave their son a peaceful death. He came under my care many years ago, when I worked in Yorkshire. He was only thirty-five, and had several admissions with liver failure. He had a degree of intellectual disability, and could not truly comprehend what was happening to him. The origins of his alcohol dependence were sad, and slightly comic. Education and work had passed him by, and the only environment where he felt truly accepted was the local pub. Although he had the mind of a child, he learned certain manly phrases, and was adopted by the hard-drinking pub regulars as a sort of mascot. He had neither the insight nor the motivation to stop drinking. During his last admission, it became clear that he would not recover. I spoke to his devoted father, and advised him that intensive care had little or nothing to offer and that we should aim for comfort. To my relief, the father agreed, and the family spent the last night at the bedside, praying. Many patients and families, however, cannot embrace what they regard as 'giving up'. Liver cirrhosis is a perfect example of how the modern practice of pushing treatment to the limit can go wrong.

BRINKMANSHIP

The American medical ethicist Daniel Callahan has defined the term 'technological brinkmanship' as:

> A powerful clinical drive to push technology as far as possible to save life while, at the same time, preserving a decent quality of life. It is well recognized by now that, if medical technology is pushed too far,

a person can be harmed, that there is a line that should not be crossed. I define "brinkmanship" as the gambling effort to go *as close to that line as possible* before the cessation or abatement of treatment.

This sounds good in theory, but Callahan identified the obvious limitation of this strategy:

In particular, brinkmanship fails to reckon with two potent realities, each of which conspires to make it hard to locate the point at which the brinkmanship should stop, and just as hard to work up the will to stop once this point has been identified. The two realities are the vanishing line between life and death, which makes it difficult to determine when to stop the use of technology, and the continuing profound public and medical ambivalence about what is wanted and valued in coping with illness and dying.

Callahan's 'vanishing line between life and death' simply refers to the difficulty in being sure, in a patient with a chronic disease, when the process of dying has started. This vanishing line, this difficulty, contributed to the demise of the Liverpool Care Pathway in 2013. Medicine is, and always has been, messy, imprecise and uncertain. And nothing is as messy, imprecise and uncertain as predicting death.

SOCIETY'S DUSTBIN?

The GP and writer Iona Heath asked: 'Why is it that so few of our patients die what would be recognized or described as a good death?' She goes on to recount a patient's story:

Some years ago, an elderly patient on my list was admitted to hospital after she collapsed. She was in her late eighties, a widow and very frail. She was admitted to a coronary care unit and received the highest possible standard of care including fibrinolytic treatment ['clot-busting' drugs] delivered according to the latest evidence-based guidelines. She made a good recovery and was discharged home, apparently well, a week later. I went to see her and found her to be very grateful for the kindness she had been shown but profoundly shocked by a course of treatment that she perceived to be completely inappropriate. She explained to me that not only her husband but almost all her generation of friends and acquaintances were already dead, that her physical frailty prevented her from doing almost all the things that she had previously enjoyed and that she had no desire to live much longer. No one had asked her about any of this or attempted to discover whether the effective and therefore recommended treatment for her condition was appropriate in her particular case. She died three weeks later while asleep in bed.

Let us for a moment examine Heath's assertion that someone should have carried out what can only be described as an existential assessment of this old lady before giving fibrinolytic treatment. The patient was almost certainly treated by a busy, shift-working junior doctor, and the old lady was one of perhaps dozens of acute patients seen on that shift. It is rather fanciful to imagine that in such circumstances, an assessment of the patient's sense of herself and her situation would be a priority. Furthermore, a decision to deny such a patient 'clot-busting' treatment could easily be construed as ageist – even the normally sensible Raymond Tallis (geriatrician and philosopher) has labelled doctors who do not treat the old as actively as they treat the young as 'scoundrels'. It is an absurd suggestion that an on-call junior doctor should take such a professional risk. Even if the old lady – after the detailed existential assessment suggested by Iona Heath – was happy to reject such treatment herself, it is not unknown for relatives to emerge after the patient's death, demanding to know why their loved one was denied potentially life-saving procedures. One can imagine the scene at the inquest:

CORONER: Doctor, why did you not give this patient, with a known myocardial infarct, fibrinolytic therapy?'

DOCTOR: Well, I had a long chat with her, and it emerged that she had lost not only her husband but almost all her generation of friends and acquaintances were already dead, that her physical frailty prevented her from doing almost all the things she had previously enjoyed and that she had no desire to live much longer. That being the case, I decided that fibrinolytic therapy was inappropriate.

The Sun newspaper reports on the case: 'Nan dies after doc denies her clot-buster'.

I admire Iona Heath: she has been an eloquent critic of the excesses of modern medicine, and her contribution to the debate on assisted suicide has been refreshing and challenging. She fails, however, to comprehend the reality of being a junior doctor on-call for a Coronary Care Unit in a busy general hospital. General practice has changed dramatically in the last twenty years or so. GPs no longer provide out-of-hours care for their own patients, as they did in the past. It is rather disingenuous of family doctors, therefore, to criticize the less than holistic care provided by hospitals when they have delegated their own out-of-hours responsibility to cooperatives and deputizing services. If Iona Heath was so concerned about her elderly patient, she could have exercised her right as the patient's GP to resist her admission to hospital and simply have treated her at home, in her own familiar environment, without the clot-busting drugs and other nasty things doled out by the uncaring hospital. The Coronary Care Unit should not be expected to provide spiritual guidance.

Heath's criticism of acute hospital care is symptomatic of a wider societal issue: acute hospitals are criticized, with some justification, for failing to care properly for the dying, yet society has handed over most of the responsibility for care of the dying to these very same hospitals. Nursing homes commonly send dying patients into emergency departments because it is much easier for them, administratively and legally, if the patient dies in hospital: no mess, no questions from troublesome relatives, no possibility of inspections by government agencies, no death certificate to fill in. Let somebody else take responsibility.

Acute hospitals have become a dustbin for all sorts of societal problems, not just dying. As a consultant on-call for acute 'unselected' General Medicine, I commonly admit elderly people whose only problem is that they can no longer live independently. I have admitted women whose only problem is a violent husband. I have even admitted an elderly man who simply wanted free accommodation while his house was being redecorated. If we, as a society, treat acute hospitals as dustbins for all sorts of non-medical problems, we should not complain if these hospitals begin to look and feel like, well, dustbins. The doctors and the hospitals did not ask for these problems – society was quite happy to hand them over, as long as the problems could be given a medical gloss. And the greatest of these problems is death. Ivan Illich assumed that 'medicalization' is something doctors actively seek, to enhance their power. But he was wrong. Medicalization does not empower doctors: they suffer.

Ireland has a long and unedifying tradition of medicalizing social problems. At one period in the mid twentieth century, the country had proportionately more people (2 per cent of the entire adult population) in long-term psychiatric care than Stalin's Soviet Union. Many of these 'patients' had no psychiatric illness as such. Some were simply troublesome: spinster sisters who needed to be got rid of to make way for the new wife on the farm, delinquent teenagers, and so on. The Irish public was quite happy with this state of affairs, although there was much public hand-wringing when the late Mary Raftery made a television documentary on the subject.

Some relatives I have dealt with believe that acute hospitals should function almost as a branch of the prison service, and detain against their will all sorts of people – mainly the elderly, but also other groups, such as alcoholics and anorexics. I find myself constantly, and wearily, telling my juniors and ward nurses that we work in a hospital, not a prison. Some years ago, an alcoholic patient of mine was discharged after treatment for a chest infection. Her family phoned me up to express their outrage that I had willingly and knowingly sent home a woman who would start drinking again. I explained that this was regrettable, but the patient had made her choice, which I had to respect. They threatened to report me to the police, the Irish Medical Council and, most tellingly, to the Joe Duffy Radio Show. (This show affords the Irish public the opportunity to let off steam about any sort of perceived injustice.) I offered to give them the contact details for all three agencies, and never heard from them again.

A seventy-year-old woman was brought in to the Emergency Department one Sunday afternoon some years ago when I was on General Medical 'take'. She lived alone, in conditions of absolute squalor, surviving somehow on a diet of cigarettes, strong tea and whiskey. The ambulance had been summoned by well-meaning, concerned neighbours and relatives. One of the ambulance crew told the medical staff in the Emergency Department that the woman lived in 'the worst conditions he had seen in twenty years'. I talked to the old woman, and concluded that there was no medical problem as such and, more importantly, that she had the mental capacity to make her own decisions. After a day or two on the ward, when she was fed and cleaned up, she told me, clearly and pointedly, that she wanted to go home – to her own squalid house, not a care home. I explained to her that I was happy for her to go, but that her neighbours and relatives might not be so happy. Anticipating trouble, I made sure that one of my geriatrician colleagues assessed her mental capacity, and he agreed that this woman was *compos mentis*. She discharged herself from hospital: I made it clear to the nurses and junior doctors that she was not to be impeded in any way – she had made her own decision on the matter.

Her neighbours and relatives viewed the acute hospital as the correct sorting-house for this woman's existential problem, or perceived problem. I reflected that they never entertained the option of going in to clean up her house themselves or cooking her a hot meal. Clearly, these were services that the state should provide. And the best way to grab the immediate attention of the state was to bundle this poor old woman into an ambulance and land her, on a Sunday afternoon, in the Emergency Department, where she would be accommodated, against her will, on a trolley. My role was that of jailer, not doctor. Inevitably, the neighbours and relatives prevailed: she was sent back into hospital by ambulance, and eventually agreed reluctantly to go from there to a nursing home.

What has all this to do with dying? My point is this: society has thrust onto doctors and hospitals the messy, intractable and insoluble aspects of life, such as old age and death. We are now also expected to police lifestyles that others disapprove of. After all my years of practice, I am still astounded that families expect me to solve the existential problem of being old and no longer independent. Many families, who know, deep in their hearts, that an elderly parent cannot continue to live independently, wait for some acute illness to occur, when this problem then becomes the hospital's. The acute illness is generally overcome in days, yet the patient may languish in hospital for months, while the paperwork governing their existential dilemma is slowly worked through.

I obstinately cling to the notion that a doctor's role is limited: our job should be the treatment of illness. When we go beyond that – when society forces us to go beyond that – we suffer. The general public, the media and politicians constantly complain about general hospitals. They would profit by looking at themselves, and by examining what they ask of such institutions.

The medicalization of death was a gradual process. Philippe Ariès listed the various historical forces that led to it, one of which was the rise of the hospital. Most hospitals in Britain and Ireland began as infirmaries attached to workhouses. Hospitals were, as George Orwell observed, where the poor and the destitute went to die.

St Finbarr's Hospital in Cork began as such a workhouse: it is now a geriatric hospital. I can recall older patients begging me not to send them to 'The Union', as the old workhouse was called. Right up to the middle of the twentieth century, wealthy people were treated at home – operations such as appendicectomies were commonly performed by surgeons in private houses. Gradually, however, hospitals – particularly the 'voluntary' ones, which were outside the control of the municipal authorities – got better and the middle classes began to go there to get treated and, eventually, to die. Cutting out an appendix on the kitchen table was no longer the acceptable standard of care. Philippe Ariès described how the hospital began to take over the community's role in the care of the dying: 'the hospital has offered families a place where they can hide the unseemly invalid whom neither the world nor they can endure… The dying man's bedroom has passed from the home to the hospital.'

Acute general hospitals provide a great critical mass, not only of doctors and nurses, but also of equipment, facilities and ancillary services. And no matter what happened at the Stafford Hospital, a large acute general hospital is still the safest place to be if you are acutely ill, especially if that illness is complex and life-threatening. GPs no longer deliver babies or set broken bones. Private hospitals, although they provide single en suite rooms, appetizing food and good parking, are no place for the acutely ill.

So: large acute general hospitals are the best place to be when you are very sick but not the ideal place in which to die. Yet that is where most of us are destined to spend our last days and hours. Is there a better option?

CHAPTER 5

Deathology

In 2013 I was invited to give a lecture – on gastrostomy (PEG) tube-feeding – at our local hospice, Marymount in Cork. After the lecture, I asked the hospice's medical director, Tony O'Brien, to show me around. I had spent the morning at my own hospital, and the contrast between the two institutions could not have been greater. The new hospice had taken decades to fund and build, and was eventually completed, despite Ireland's economic collapse. It is difficult to convey just how physically impressive the building is: all is light, glass, polished blond wood, a cross between a luxury hotel and the headquarters of a multinational corporation. It is the most architecturally impressive hospital I have ever been in, an honour which before I visited Marymount had gone to the National Cancer Centre Hospital in Tokyo. Order and good humour abounds: no rushing trolleys, no funny smells. A huge atrium is filled with plants and running water. All the rooms are single and en suite. There is a bright and airy prayer room. There are designated areas for hairdressers, art classes and natural healers. The staff certainly look very happy, and palliative care has no difficulty recruiting trainees.

The new hospice gives an impression of club-class death, but Tony O'Brien is sensitive to the perception that hospices provide 'de-luxe' dying. He pointed out to me that at any one time, his service has forty in-patients at the hospice, but ten times that number on their books in the general hospitals and in the community. He is also exasperated by the notion that palliative care is exclusively about care of the dying. 'I care for the living and the dying,' he told me. He is right: palliative care doctors look after the dying, certainly, but also care for many others with chronic illnesses that cannot be cured.

It wasn't always like this. Palliative, or hospice, care was essentially invented by one woman: Cicely Saunders. She had trained as a nurse, but went on to qualify as a doctor, having been advised by the surgeon Norman Barrett that if she wanted to work with the dying, she should study medicine, because it was doctors who deserted the dying. She had what were then radical ideas about the care of the dying, and set up the first hospice in London, St Christopher's. In the early years, hospices dealt almost exclusively with patients dying of cancer and the discipline was then known as 'terminal care'. Hospital doctors were suspicious, and defensive, about the need for such a specialty. They (correctly) perceived it as a judgment on their shortcomings: palliative care arose from a real need to improve treatment of the dying. Generations of palliative care specialists, including Tony O'Brien, subsequently trained at St Christopher's. Tony came back to Cork in the early 1990s and became the first specialist palliative care physician in the region, when he joined the staff at the old Marymount Hospice, a rambling Victorian building near the city centre.

You do not need a medical background to see immediately that the new Marymount Hospice offers a peaceful, decorous and dignified environment for dying people. Yet the fact remains that ten times as many deaths take place in the acute hospitals. This may be in part down to a simple lack of capacity, with limited access to hospice beds, but it also reflects, I believe, an unwillingness on the part of the sick and the dying to embrace the relatively new rituals of the hospice. By that I mean that patients receiving treatment from the hospice have accepted, to a greater or lesser extent, that their condition is not curable, and that, sooner or later, they will die from it. Many of my patients are unwilling to accept or make this judgment, and by the time they do, it is too late, and they die in the acute general hospital. Tony told me that the families of some of his patients dying at Marymount don't mention the hospice's name in the newspaper death notice (so important in Ireland), because dying in a hospice is still seen by some as vaguely shameful.

It needs to be said that it is easier for hospices to look good compared to acute general hospitals. By the time the dying patient has embraced the hospice ritual, the hard work – namely, altering their expectation of the future – has already been done by another doctor. When a patient is admitted to a hospice, there are no longer questions about ICU admission, further investigations or more chemotherapy. The hospice doctors work at a less frenetic pace than their colleagues in the general hospitals; 'saving lives' is not part of their job description. The environment of the hospice is notable for the absence of chaos, squalor, frayed tempers and shabbiness.

Most dying patients, however, never get to embrace hospice care, and most deaths still take place in acute hospitals and nursing homes. For some, hospice care is tantamount to surrender, to 'giving up'. I am reminded of a patient, an elderly man with advanced and incurable cancer. I went to see him one morning and spoke with him and his son. It was clear to me that he was dying. I tentatively suggested that we should consider admission to the hospice. His son asked to speak to me outside his room and told me that he was appalled: I had dared to use what she called 'the M word' (Marymount) in the man's presence. For some, even speaking the name of the hospice is tantamount to giving up. I was forced into making an abject and unconditional apology.

Dying patients do not seem to move in an orderly fashion through Elisabeth Kübler-Ross's five neat stages of denial, anger, bargaining, depression and acceptance. Many never get past denial. Some jump straight to depression. Others do it in reverse; and some rebels don't do any of the five stages. Hospice care is a different ritual to hospital care, and many patients are unwilling or unable to embrace this ritual. It is quite a cultural leap from the oncology unit to the hospice. It was not a leap that Susan Sontag or Christopher Hitchens, for example, would have made, but more about that later.

HAPPY AT HOME?

Dying at home has become a kind of middle-class ideal, but may not be suitable for everyone. Many patients and their families cannot cope at home if the illness ravages them with incontinence, confusion, terror and pain. Ann McPherson, who died in 2011, was a GP and a prominent campaigner for assisted suicide. She died of pancreatic cancer, and her daughter Tess, a dermatologist, described her mother's death (at home) in an article for the *British Medical Journal*:

> On the final day the doctor was getting the syringe drivers ready when something changed in my mum's breathing. The nurse explained that she would die soon and left us. We were with mum, and that was what she wanted. As she died her body seemed furious with its final fight, gasping to the end. With a desperate haunting shudder from mum I found myself sitting in pools of expelled fluid. That was not what she wanted. Mum had seen this happen before and wanted it avoided for future patients and their families. It is simple: the law needs to change to allow terminally ill but mentally competent people the right to a more dignified death than my mum was allowed.

Whatever one's view on the law (which I will examine later), I was struck after reading this piece that Ann McPherson should have died in a hospice, not at home. Having doctors in the family is not always an advantage – dermatology may not be the ideal professional background for such a task. McPherson's daughter could not assess the situation objectively and may have felt a pressure to care for her mother herself at home, when hospice admission was clearly required. Perhaps what

Ann McPherson needed was for a hospice to take over, not a change in the law.

Raymond Tallis became chairman of Healthcare Professionals for Assisted Dying (HPAD) after McPherson's death. He believes that a minority of dying people are 'suffering unbearably, despite receiving optimal palliative care'. He argues that starvation and dehydration and continuous sedation are ploys used to get around the prohibition on assisted dying, and are a 'clinical, ethical and legal fudge'. It pains me to disagree with Tallis, since I admire him so much, but I cannot recall a single patient, in over thirty years of practice at the front line, who I wished I had been able to 'assist'.

My father-in-law died at home in October 2013. His condition had deteriorated rapidly over that autumn, and by late September the local GP practice nurses installed a hospital bed in the front room of his house. He was relieved to take to the bed, and never left it, dying two weeks later. My wife had travelled to Scotland on many weekends over the year after his diagnosis, and was there for her father's final weeks. I arrived with our two children two days before he died. By that time, he had been started on morphine, given slowly and steadily by the syringe-driver, mainly for his pain, but also for terror. When we arrived, he was semi-conscious. He struggled on for two more days, his breathing becoming more and more laboured. There were frequent episodes of apnoea (when breathing temporarily stops); when he finally died, we weren't sure initially if this wasn't just another apnoeic attack. (This pattern of breathing in the dying is known as Cheyne-Stokes respiration, after the two Dublin physicians who described it.)

My father-in-law managed to die at home, but I'm not sure if that was what he wanted. He hated the thought of his grandchildren seeing their once omnipotent Papa so diminished. There were episodes when his body let him down, which were deeply distressing to him. His wife, exhausted and bewildered, accompanied him to the end. His dying at home was partly dictated by the fact that there was no local hospice, only a designated ward in the local district general hospital.

Although a small minority of people in Britain and Ireland die in a hospice, half of all people dying in the US do so. Intriguingly, and predictably, money is the main reason. A now-famous study from the Massachusetts General Hospital randomly assigned patients with stage IV lung cancer to two types of treatment. Half of the patients had the standard cancer (oncology) care, half had standard cancer care combined with palliative (hospice) care. The patients who had the combined oncology/palliative care did better in every conceivable way: they stopped chemotherapy sooner, they were admitted to a hospice earlier, they were much less likely to have interventionist treatment or ICU admission near the end of life, and they lived, on average, 25 per cent longer. What interested the US medical insurance companies – usually the baddies in any of these stories – was that the patients who had combined care cost them much less. The insurers now actively encourage their customers to embrace hospice care at the end of life.

A study published in the *Journal of the American Medical Association* in 2013 found that, in 2009, 33.5 per cent of Medicare beneficiaries died at home, a 10 per cent increase compared to 2000. Forty-two per cent died in hospice care (nearly twice the percentage in 2000), and 24.6 per cent died in hospital (from 32.6 per cent in 2000). It's not all good news, however:

> ...the rate of ICU use in the last month of life has increased, with 29.2% of decedents experiencing an ICU in the last months of life in 2009. Another indicator of change in end-of-life medical care is that 11.5% of 2009 decedents had 3 or more hospitalizations in the last 90 days of life. Hospice use increased, but 28.4% of those decedents used a hospice for 3 days or less in 2009. About one-third of these short hospice stays were preceded by an ICU stay in the last month of life.

The dying experienced an average of three 'transitions' from one healthcare setting to another in the last 90 days of life: 14 per cent were moved in the last three days of life. All we can conclude from these data is that knowing where a person died tells us very little about the quality of care received by that person. These statistics also reflect, I believe, the phenomenon of what I call the negative currency of responsibility: the less of it you have, the better. One of the main motivators of behaviour of healthcare professionals (particularly doctors) is the evasion of this currency. The burden – our dirty little secret – now so great, is best described by Raymond Tallis's memorable phrase 'the unbearable heaviness of responsibility'.

DIGNITY AND NARRATIVE

Palliative care uses a different vocabulary to other medical specialties, one that suggests an expanded role beyond mere symptom control. In the past, the specialty has been accused of over-emphasis on symptom control, at the expense of what might be called metaphysical issues. North American palliative care physicians have attempted to quantify these metaphysical issues with the 'Patient Dignity Inventory' (PDI), designed to measure sources of 'dignity-related distress' among dying patients. This Inventory is designed to form the basis for dignity therapy – encompassing the patient's life, their achievements, their hopes and their fears. 'Dignity therapy', opines

Harvey Max Chochinov, a Canadian psychiatrist, 'should be delivered by a skilled and sensitive clinician who, guided by a core set of questions, maintains sufficient flexibility to follow in the direction of the patient. Using a supportive-expressive approach to the clinical encounter, the personal needs of the patient are paramount to the therapeutic process.' The Patient Dignity Inventory consists of five factors:

1. Symptom distress (physically distressing symptoms, feeling depressed, anxious, and uncertain, being worried about the future, not being able to think clearly).

2. Existential distress (feeling that how you look has changed, that you are no longer who you were, not feeling worthwhile or valued, not being able to carry out important roles, feeling that life no longer has meaning or purpose, feeling that you are a burden to others).

3. Dependency (not being able to perform the tasks of daily living, not being able to attend to bodily functions, reduced privacy).

4. Peace of mind (feeling you have not made a meaningful contribution, a sense of unfinished business, concerns regarding spiritual life).

5. Social support (not feeling supported by friends or family, not feeling supported by health care providers, not being treated with respect).

A pretty tough list, I thought. Most conversations I have had with the dying do not get past factor one, symptom distress. In fact, I'm lucky if I get that far with most patients. And I'm not sure, if I were the dying patient, that I would want to discuss most of these issues with a physician, no matter how 'skilled and sensitive' the inquisitor. I am not at all convinced that these are problems a doctor should be addressing: is it really any business of mine if my patient has worries about his legacy, or his relationship with God? These are dilemmas that are more appropriately discussed with family, close friends and (perhaps) a chaplain, without the intervention of a 'skilful and sensitive' medical facilitator. As early as the mid-1970s, Philippe Ariès feared that the (then) new hospice movement was taking over roles and functions which up until then had been the province of family and priest.

Dignity therapy is closely related to 'narrative medicine', another American movement. The term 'narrative medicine' was coined by Rita Charon, Professor of Clinical Medicine at Columbia University Medical Center, New York. The programme in Narrative Medicine there has as its mission statement: 'Narrative medicine fortifies clinical practice with the narrative competence to recognize, absorb, metabolize, interpret and be moved by the stories of illness.'

Like the narrative medicine movement, palliative care sometimes seems to speak in a different language, one that can be marked, as I have said, by a kind of cloying earnestness, or 'chronic niceness' as the hospital chaplain Peter Speck called it. A paper by M. K. Kearney and others, 'Self-care of Physicians Caring for Patients at the End of Life', recommends some self-awareness practices in the workplace, to prevent professional burnout: 'As I wash my hands, I say to myself, "May the universal life-force enable me to treat my patients and colleagues with compassion, patience, and respect"... Take half a minute of silence or take turns to choose and read a poem at the beginning of weekly interdisciplinary team meetings.'

Ivan Illich raged against the medicalization of death; he would not be surprised, I think, by the emergence of dignity therapy and narrative medicine, with doctors taking on a quasi-sacerdotal role and assuming concerns for matters which, in the past, were regarded as 'spiritual', not 'medical'. Tellingly, Illich called modern scientific medicine a 'monolithic world religion'.

BREAKING BAD NEWS

'Breaking bad news' is now regarded as a special skill, best practised by palliative care specialists. The paradox in this assertion is that, in order for patients to engage with a palliative care specialist, they need to already know that they have a lethal disease. As I explained earlier, if I arrange for an oncologist to see one of my patients, the onus is on me to tell the patient that he or she has cancer. As I have argued, there is no good way of breaking bad news, but there are many bad ways to do it. My own practice, the result of many years of trial and error, is this: get everyone – patient, family, nurses – together. Try to find a quiet room, if you can. 'Ambience', a colleague once remarked, 'is more important than words.' Families frequently express disappointment with this arrangement: often, they want me to give them the complete and unedited information first, and then a much-diluted (and censored) version to the patient. Not uncommonly, the various relatives ask to be talked to individually, and in detail. It is infinitely preferable for all concerned to hear the same information: this approach dramatically reduces the potential for misinformation, confusion and conflict. News, it has been said, is neither good nor bad: it depends on the perspective of the recipient. For example, a very sick person might regard a short prognosis as 'good' news – the end is in sight. 'Bad' news is often swiftly forgotten, or denied. I have several patients who, following the Difficult Conversation, talk to me the next day in a manner which suggests the conversation never took place.

Atul Gawande interviewed Dr Susan Block, a palliative care specialist at his (Gawande's) own hospital, the Brigham and Women's in Boston: 'Block is a nationally recognized pioneer in training doctors and others in managing end-of-life issues with patients and families. "You have to understand", Block told me, "A family meeting is a *procedure* [my italics], and it requires no less skill than performing an operation."' Apart from the self-regard of this assertion, it is indicative of a rather worrying trend: namely, the notion that palliative care specialists such as Block are the most skilled and best trained to have the Difficult Conversation. I do not believe that doctors can be taught to do this. There are as many different Difficult Conversations as there are patients. It is a private mystery that only many years of practice teaches.

I noticed the same phenomenon in a 2009 article in the *New York Times* about palliative care. The acknowledged star of the article is an Irish palliative care specialist, Sean O'Mahony. The author of the piece, the rather splendidly named Anemona Hartocollis, was clearly quite taken by O'Mahony: 'Dr O'Mahony favors crisp button-down shirts, but no white coat. His bedside manner ranges from gentle amusement to studied neutrality; he eerily resembles the un-emotive Steve McQueen of *Bullit* [sic].' She goes on to describe an encounter with a cancer patient:

Deborah Migliore was pushed into a small conference room in a wheelchair, looking kittenish in red and white pajamas and big gold hoop earrings. Her weight was down to about 90 pounds, from 116, her face gaunt, her sad eyes droopier than ever.

Dr Sean O'Mahony had been called in to tell her the bad news: she was sicker than she realized, and the prognosis did not look good...

Part psychoanalyst, part detective, Dr O'Mahony had to listen to the cues and decide what to do next.

Most doctors do not excel at delivering bad news, decades of studies show, if only because it goes against their training to save lives, not end them. But Dr O'Mahony, who works at Montefiore Medical Center in the Bronx, belongs to a class of doctors, known as palliative care specialists, who have made death their life's work. They study how to deliver bad news, and they do it again and again. They know secrets like who, as a rule, takes it better. They know who is more likely to suffer silently, and when is the best time to suggest a do-not-resuscitate order.

Why, I wonder, did Deborah Migliore's oncologist delegate the unpleasant task of breaking the bad news to a palliative care specialist, even one as skilled and charismatic as Sean O'Mahony? It strikes me as an extraordinary dereliction of duty to delegate this difficult, and sometimes unpleasant, task, to a doctor who may hitherto have had nothing to do with the patient. I suspect this happens because American oncologists are expected by their patients to be relentlessly up-beat and optimistic. How wonderfully, and typically, American – to delegate the unpleasant duty of breaking bad news to another physician, skilled in Difficult Conversations, a specialist in 'deathology'.

THE BLACK BOX

There is much confusion about syringe-drivers. Families of dying patients commonly view the setting up of the 'black box' as a prelude to imminent death. A syringe-driver is simply a means of delivering medication, nothing more. Typically, a painkiller (usually morphine), a sedative and a drug to reduce excessive secretions are given in combination. It does not hasten death; it does not mean that the doctors have 'given up'. Tony O'Brien recalled a relative who made this Freudian slip: 'Doctor, are you going to start the *gun* – I mean *driver*?'

I do not blame relatives for thinking like this: patients on a syringe-driver rarely live beyond forty-eight hours, even if the driver does not actually hasten death. The period after its setting up is rather strange: the patient usually attains a calmness and peace, drifting in and out of consciousness. Families usually maintain an around-the-clock vigil. 'Agony' is now a word used to describe the emotions of football fans whose team has lost a cup final in extra time, or the physical discomfort associated with certain types of dental treatment. It used to mean the final stages of a difficult or painful death. Geoffrey Gorer used the word in its original meaning: 'Questioning my old acquaintances, I cannot find one over the age of sixty who did not witness the agony of at least one near relative; I do not think I know a single person under the age of thirty who has had a similar experience.' Doctors still use the word 'agonal' to describe the irregular and laboured breathing of those nearing death: this phenomenon, as mentioned earlier, is also called Cheyne-Stokes respiration. Old-fashioned Christians contemplate the Agony of the Cross; indeed, the final agony of ordinary people was once thought to be mysterious, grand and awesome. The syringe-driver allows for a softer, less frightening, final agony, or abolishes it completely.

BRINGING IT ALL BACK HOME

Medical education is still almost exclusively focused on diagnosis and treatment, and not enough on 'outcomes' – the results of treatment. To take an example from my line of work, patients admitted to hospital with liver failure have a high mortality. Yet the textbooks of liver disease have little to say about the complex emotional and ethical difficulties encountered when these (mainly young) patients are dying. The books and journals seem almost afraid to tackle such issues, as if to do so would be an admission of failure.

Care of the dying needs to return to the core of what doctors do, and should not become the exclusive preserve of palliative care specialists, no matter how caring, intuitive and charismatic they may be. And this care should be practical, delivered by a doctor who knows the patient. The dying need more than well-intentioned, unfocused sympathy. Dying from liver disease, for example, can be messy and complex, and there are eventualities and complications (bleeding, fluid collections within the abdomen, and so on) that are best dealt with by a liver specialist. There is some evidence that professional bodies are waking up to this fact: for example, the British Association for the Study of the Liver has admitted that palliative and end-of-life care is one of the greatest unmet needs for patients with liver disease. I welcome, and regularly request, advice from my palliative care colleagues, but I do not do so with the intention of getting rid of my dying patients.

Paradoxically, your patient needs you most when they are dying. Like many other doctors, I have tended in the past to move quickly on from the dying patient on ward rounds, pausing briefly to check with the nurse that they are 'comfortable'. Studies have shown that when patients are classified as 'DNACPR' (Do Not Attempt Cardio-Pulmonary Resuscitation), the frequency of visits from their doctor declines. It is almost as if we are ashamed to acknowledge our 'failures'. This is, of course, absurd, but it reflects how doctors have been trained, and what we learned from our bosses. And it isn't just sympathy that the dying need, but also practical things: pain relief, of course, but also relief from itching, nausea, breathlessness and terror. The palliative care specialists are, indeed, expert at symptom relief, but patients tend to trust the doctors they know. When I qualified as a doctor thirty years ago, it was quite common for a patient's GP to visit him or her in hospital. This is now almost unheard of, which is a shame, for the hospital staff could learn something about the patient from a doctor who has known the individual for many years.

I am a supporter of the concept of hospice care. I believe, however, that 'palliative care' should be at the centre of what *all* doctors do. It should not be something that we delegate to death-specialists when we, the techno-logical doctors, have run out of ideas and potential treatments. 'Breaking bad news' and having the Difficult Conversation is part of the job and cannot become the exclusive preserve of specialists in bad news and Difficult Conversations. I may not be as skilled, or as sensitive as Susan Block or Sean O'Mahony, but my patients should hear it from me. The doctor who knows the patient best – *their* doctor – is the right doctor to accompany him or her on the way to death, to be their *amicus mortis*.

Several years ago, a man in his mid-sixties was admitted, as an emergency patient, under my care with chest pain and shortness of breath. He lived alone, in a remote rural area. He had been undergoing treatment (radiation and chemotherapy) for cancer. This treatment had been agreed and coordinated by a special cancer multidisciplinary team, which included a surgeon, a radiation specialist and an oncologist. The chest X-ray I ordered showed cancer deposits throughout both lungs. On my next ward round, the man asked me what was happening, what did the X-rays show? I told him. 'How could this be?' he asked me. 'My doctor told me the chances of cure were nearly 100 per cent!' He was dismayed that he had been abandoned by the doctors ('the multidisciplinary team') who had treated him for several months, and that the unpleasant task of telling him the truth had been foisted on a doctor he had first met two days ago.

I KNOW HOW YOU FEEL:
EMPATHY AND KINDNESS

Medical schools are now expected to impart communication skills and foster empathy. But can we teach empathy? Narrative medicine claims to do so. As an example of narrative medicine in practice, Rita Charon cites an encounter with a woman with Charcot-Marie-Tooth disease, a hereditary neurological disorder. She learns that the patient's seven-year-old son has started to show signs of the disease, and she is 'engulfed by sadness as she listens to her patient... the physician grieves along with the patient, aware of how disease changes everything, what it means, what it claims, how random is its unfairness, and how much courage it takes to look it full in the face'. We learn that, in a subsequent visit, Charon gives the patient a piece she has written about their previous encounter and reports that the patient 'felt relieved that her physician seemed to understand her pain'. 'She can listen at a different level,' says an admirer. Practitioners and students of narrative medicine are encouraged to see the clinical consultation as a story, set against a complex backdrop of personal history, culture, ethnicity, gender and economic status. Students are taught the skills of 'narrative competency'. Literature is mined for examples of the experience of illness. Reading and writing groups encourage students and doctors to write their own narratives about their patients and their jobs, and they may even – à la Rita Charon – encourage patients to read what they have written about them.

The narrative medicine movement has achieved pre-eminence within the field of medical humanities.

For many within the medical profession, however, narrative medicine provokes mockery and contempt for its smugness, its pretension and its risible, strangely biblical jargon ('honouring', 'witnessing', 'professing'). It encourages doctors to stray from their core professional duties into uncharted waters, to take on roles such as spiritual adviser, social worker, life-coach, friend. Vulnerable patients may develop unrealistic expectations of doctors, hopes that will inevitably be disappointed. And it is not only patients who lose out. Impressionable medical students may feel themselves to be failures if they do not manage to match the superhuman empathy of a Rita Charon. Doctors who are not 'engulfed with sadness', or who fail to 'grieve' with their patients, may be encouraged to undergo training in 'narrative competency'. Doctors should – and generally do – treat their patients with courtesy, dignity and kindness. It is inevitable that they sometimes fall short in this regard and fail to show grace under the intense pressure of modern practice. The narrative medicine imperative to express an empathy which the doctor may or may not feel cheapens, undermines and coarsens the relationship between patient and doctor. Older, more stoically inclined patients in particular may find this form of engagement with their doctor vulgar, embarrassing and intrusive.

'Empathy' implies that we can feel what someone else is feeling, which, of course, we generally can't.

Kindness is different: it is possible, for example, to be kind to someone one doesn't feel empathy with. Kindness is a more honest currency; it was the ingredient that was most singularly lacking in the care of patients at Stafford Hospital.

I have seen enough of the kind of death that happens in acute hospitals to know that, when my time comes, I will embrace wholeheartedly the rituals of hospice care and place myself in the tender care of Marymount Hospice. I will gladly accept the ministrations of natural healers and kinesiologists. I will, if I am able, attend art classes. I will pray to whatever God is listening to me. I will not be slow in asking for morphine. I will not, however, expect the doctors there to ask me about my existential anxieties, or to engage with me on my spiritual life.

Palliative care – and medicine generally – is often accused of 'medicalizing' death. But a certain degree of medicalization is necessary. The correct use of drugs and the relief of distressing symptoms are skills that doctors (particularly palliative care doctors) bring to the care of the dying. What I have argued against is *over-*medicalization of dying. Palliative care has achieved much since Cicely Saunders opened the hospice at St Christopher's: many people were relieved of suffering that was commonplace in the relatively recent past. But the specialty somehow stands outside, rather than within, the medical mainstream.

I recently dined with an old friend, who worked for many years as a palliative care physician. She is ambivalent about the specialty: 'The notion of a "good death" is endlessly debated as something desirable and achievable. Yet this notion is hugely subjective, poorly understood, and quite probably not a generalizable concept. How we die reflects how we live, and palliative care has, I believe, misguidedly set the "good death" as its guiding aim.' My friend also admits ruefully to believing that, when she entered the specialty in the late 1980s, its success would eventually lead to its demise: if all doctors were properly educated in care of the dying and the relief of suffering in people with incurable disease, specialists in palliative care would no longer be required. She reflected: 'I was wrong. Palliative care has become a powerful force in its own right, one that has achieved and continues to achieve so much in terms of the relief of suffering for so many. Yet I remain troubled. The speciality increasingly sees itself as exclusively all-knowing, and territorial, about how we die.'

CHAPTER 6

Celebrity Cancer Ward

Death from cancer is qualitatively different from death due to other causes, so much so, that up until quite recently, hospices cared almost exclusively for people dying from this disease (or diseases). Dying of cancer, of course, is no more unpleasant than dying of, say, heart failure or emphysema. In fact, death from cancer may be *better* than death from other diseases. The *Quality Standards for End-of-Life Care in Hospitals* from the Hospice Friendly Hospitals Programme in Ireland summarized the findings of an audit: 'A hierarchy exists in the quality of dying in Irish hospitals, based on the patient's disease. The range, from best to worst, is: cancer, circulatory diseases, respiratory diseases, dementia/frailty.' Richard Smith, former editor of the *British Medical Journal*, provoked outrage when, in 2014, he made the same observation and suggested that we should 'stop wasting billions trying to cure cancer'.

The most feared of all diseases, cancer used to be unmentionable and was called 'the big C'. Now, we hear about it constantly. We are urged to assist the 'fight against cancer' by 'raising awareness' or by donating money. We are reminded that famous, rich and talented people get cancer too, and their experiences are commonly shared with us, by themselves or by their survivors. Even the language is different: people afflicted with the condition are expected to 'fight' it; when they die, they are said to have 'lost their battle'. Cancer is seen as an alien invader, which reflects the vocabulary of the disease: 'spreading', 'metastasizing', 'invasive', 'aggressive', 'riddled'. And cancer also carries the stigma for patients of having brought it on themselves, by smoking, drinking too much alcohol, eating a bad diet or being overweight. Cancer inspires more fears and fantasies than any other cause of disease and death.

Simon Hoggart was diagnosed with pancreatic cancer in June 2010. Hoggart, a parliamentary sketch writer with the *Guardian*, was a witty journalist, who also chaired BBC Radio 4's *The News Quiz* and wrote amusingly about wine for the *Spectator*. His father Richard, who survived

Simon by three months, was a distinguished academic and cultural commentator, author of the landmark *The Uses of Literacy*. Simon, for all his talents, devoted his energies to more frivolous projects.

Pancreatic cancer has a dismal prognosis: most patients are dead within a year of diagnosis. Hoggart's cancer had spread to his spleen and lungs by the time he was diagnosed, but he survived for three and a half years, having had 'cutting-edge' treatment at the Royal Marsden Hospital in London. Unusually, Hoggart made the decision not to publicize his condition. His daughter Amy wrote in the *Guardian* after his death:

> 'You've got to get a joke out of it' was the main piece of advice he gave me about writing. In the end, his big idea was for a TV show idea called 'Celebrity Cancer Ward', inspired by the few well-known figures he bumped into during treatment. Dad would host it and each episode would track the progress of the well-known contributors' progress [*sic*]. Unsurprisingly, this was never seriously pitched. But I'm mentioning it in print here, so we will all know whose idea it originally was if it ever gets made, which it shouldn't.

It is entirely possible that such a show *could* get made; reality TV has reached parts of human experience we never thought would be presented to us as entertainment, and people's willingness to sacrifice their privacy and dignity is truly astonishing. Hoggart did not want to be defined by this illness, and deliberately chose not to follow the example of other famous cancer victims, such as John Diamond, Philip Gould, Christopher Hitchens and Jenny Diski: 'I didn't want people thinking of me as Cancer Victim, Simon Hoggart, smiling through his pain.'

CHRISTOPHER HITCHENS: 'A RADICAL, CHILDLIKE HOPE'

Christopher Hitchens had been a prolific journalist and public intellectual for more than three decades when he finally achieved the global fame he so richly deserved following the publication of *God Is Not Great* in 2007. 'Hitch' had been a swaggering figure in literary and political circles for many years before this. He was a provocative polemicist who savaged the reputations of Henry Kissinger, Bill Clinton and Mother Teresa. A brilliant speaker and debater, he had the gift of the immediate and apposite retort. (Simon Hoggart had advised him, early in his career, to 'write more like you talk'.) He moved to the US in the 1980s. After the success of *God Is Not Great*, Hitchens joined the premier league of celebrity atheist intellectuals. While Richard Dawkins was perceived as arrogant, humourless and hectoring, even his opponents admired Hitchens's wit, his preternatural fluency and his cheek. Although wildly inconsistent and self-contradictory, he never confessed to a moment's doubt.

When Hitchens was diagnosed with oesophageal cancer, it came as no great surprise, the major risk factors for the condition being smoking and heavy drinking, both of which he cheerfully admitted to: 'Knowingly burning the candle at both ends and finding that it often gives a lovely light... I have now succumbed to something so predictable and banal that it bores even me.' His 'rackety, bohemian life' finally caught up with him in June 2010 when, during a tour to promote his memoir, *Hitch-22*, he was taken acutely ill in his hotel bedroom ('feeling as if I were actually shackled to my own corpse'), whisked off to the nearest emergency room and diagnosed with stage IV oesophageal cancer ('the thing about Stage Four is that there is no such thing as Stage Five'): the cancer had spread, or metastasized, to his lungs and the lymph nodes in his neck. Following this diagnosis, Hitchens wrote a series of articles about his illness for *Vanity Fair*, to which he had been a contributor for many years. These articles were collected, edited and book-ended by moving tributes from his wife Carol Blue and his editor Graydon Carter. This little book is simply called *Mortality*.

Hitchens's beliefs about his advanced cancer and its treatment were, for a man whose fame rested on his scepticism, uncharacteristically optimistic. While he admitted that he would be very lucky to survive, he steadfastly hoped, right to the end, that his particular case of advanced cancer might lie on the right side of the bell-shaped curve of survival statistics. He famously mocked religious folk for their faith in supernatural entities and survival of the soul after bodily death, yet the views expressed in *Mortality* are just as wishful. 'The oncology bargain', wrote Hitchens, 'is that in return for at least the chance of a few more useful years, you agree to submit to chemotherapy and then, if you are lucky with that, to radiation or even surgery.' Over the years, I have diagnosed many patients with oesophageal cancer. 'Years' is a word not generally used when discussing prognosis in stage IV oesophageal cancer; 'months', in my experience, is a more pertinent term.

Although Hitchens was bracingly dismissive of the absurd notion of 'battling cancer', he was childlike in his enthusiasm for modern American oncology: 'For example, I was encouraged to learn of a new "immunotherapy protocol", evolved by Drs Steven Rosenberg and Nicholas Restifo at the National Cancer Institute. Actually, the word "encouraged" is an understatement. I was hugely excited.' He contacts Dr Restifo, who responds enthusiastically: 'Some of this may sound like space-age medicine, but we have treated well over 100 patients with gene-engineered T cells, and have treated over 20 patients with the exact approach that I am suggesting may be applicable to your case.' Hitchens's hopes were dashed, however, when it turned out that his immune cells did not express a particular molecule (HLA-A2) which must be present for this pioneering treatment to work: 'I can't forget the feeling of flatness that I experienced when I received the news.'

His hopes were raised again when he was emailed by 'perhaps fifty friends' about a television programme called *60 Minutes*, which 'had run a segment about the "tissue engineering", by way of stem cells, of a man with a cancerous esophagus. He had effectively been medically enabled to "grow" a new one.' Hitchens's friend, Francis Collins, molecular biologist and devout Christian, head of the Human Genome Project, 'gently but firmly told me that my cancer had spread too far beyond my esophagus to be treatable by such a means'. Ironically, it is the Christian who had to lower the expectations of the sceptical atheist. Hitchens proposed to Collins that his entire DNA, along with that of his tumour, be 'sequenced', 'even though its likely efficacy lies at the outer limits of probability'. Collins was circumspect, conceding that if such 'sequencing' was performed, 'it could be clearly determined what mutations were present in the cancer that is causing it to grow. The potential for discovering mutations in the cancer cells that could lead to a new therapeutic idea is uncertain – that is at the very frontier of cancer research right now.' Collins pointed out a more prosaic reason for not having his genome 'sequenced', namely that 'the cost of having it done is also very steep at the moment'.

Mortality contains vintage Hitchensian demolitions of such received wisdoms as 'battling' cancer:

> People don't have cancer: they are reported to be battling cancer. No well-wisher omits the combative image: You can beat this. It's even in obituaries for cancer losers, as if one might reasonably say of someone that they died after a long and brave struggle with mortality. You don't hear it about long-term sufferers from heart disease or kidney failure.

He dismissed this notion of struggle: 'the image of the ardent soldier or revolutionary is the very last one that will occur to you. You feel swamped with passivity and impotence: dissolving in powerlessness like a sugar lump in water.' An admirer of Nietzsche, he came to realize that the dictum 'that which doesn't kill me makes me stronger' is nonsense: 'In the brute physical world, and the one encompassed by medicine, there are all too many things that could kill you, don't kill you, and then leave you considerably weaker.' Despite this, Hitchens remained optimistic, and he was strongly encouraged in his optimism: 'An enormous number of secular and atheist friends have told me encouraging and flattering things like, "If anyone can beat this, you can", "Cancer has no chance against someone like you"; "We know you can vanquish this".' His wife Carol Blue and his closest friend Martin Amis shared this optimism. Amis, interviewed some months after Hitchens's death, answered a question about his reasons for moving to New York: 'At this point, it looked as though Christopher might well live for *five or ten years more* [my italics].'

Mortality closes with an Afterword by Carol Blue, who writes: 'Christopher was aiming to be among the 5 to 20 per cent of those who could be cured (the odds depended on what doctor we talked to and how they interpreted the scans).' I wonder how his doctors could have given a man with stage IV oesophageal cancer such expectations of long-term survival, let alone a one in five chance of cure (which is about the survival chances for *all* oesophageal cancers, the lucky ones being those with very early, localized disease, not those with metastases in their lungs and lymph nodes). Carol Blue continues: 'Without ever deceiving himself about his medical condition, and without ever allowing me to entertain illusions about his prospects for survival, he responded to every bit of clinical and statistical good news with a radical, childlike hope.'

Hitchens recalled the absurd quixotic optimism of the Nixon-era 'War on Cancer', when America, fresh from conquering the moon, decided that the 'big C' was next. Nixon officially declared war on cancer in 1971, and confidently predicted 'complete victory' by 1976. No matter that declaring war on cancer makes as much sense as declaring war on death. No matter that cancer is not one, but hundreds of different diseases. Hitchens quoted a wickedly funny line from Updike's *Rabbit Redux*, where Mr Angstrom Senior declares: 'they're just about to lick cancer anyway and with these transplants pretty soon they can replace your whole insides.' He is assailed with well-meaning suggestions: 'in Tumortown you sometimes feel that you may expire from sheer *advice*'. He is wonderfully dismissive of 'natural' therapies: 'I did get a kind note from a Cheyenne-Arapaho friend of mine, saying that everyone she knew who had resorted to tribal remedies had died almost immediately, and suggesting that if I was offered any Native American medicines I should "move as fast as possible in the opposite direction".'

A correspondent from an (unnamed) university advised Hitchens to have himself 'cryogenically frozen against the day when the magic bullet, or whatever it is, has been devised'. This particular nonsense is a rather spooky modern echo of the Christian belief in resurrection, a parallel that Hitchens surprisingly failed to spot.

Inevitably, somebody as well connected as Hitchens was advised to see the top man (or woman): 'Extremely well-informed people also get in touch to insist that there is really only one doctor, or only one clinic.' (A contemporary equivalent of the medieval visitations to holy shrines and relics?) He admits that he did take up this advice: 'The citizens of Tumortown are forever assailed with cures and rumors of cures. I actually did take myself to one grand *palazzo* of a clinic in the richer part of the stricken city, which I will not name because all I got from it was a long and dull exposition of what I already knew...'

Only a man with stage IV cancer himself could, with impunity, skewer the sickly sentimentality of the late Randy Pausch's *The Last Lecture* (2008). Pausch, a professor of computer science at Carnegie Mellon University, was diagnosed with terminal pancreatic cancer and became an Internet sensation after his lecture was posted on YouTube. The lecture, delivered to a standing ovation at his university, was entitled 'Really Achieving Your Childhood Dreams'. Pausch also treated his audience to a demonstration of his press-up technique. Hitchens was unmoved: 'It ought to be an offence to be excruciating and unfunny in circumstances where your audience is almost morally obliged to enthuse.'

The late philosopher Sidney Hook was Hitchens's anti-Pausch. Hook, taken seriously ill in old age, 'began to reflect on the paradox that... he was able to avail himself of a historically unprecedented level of care, while at the same time being exposed to a degree of suffering that previous generations might not have been able to afford'. Hook, suffering from heart failure and a stroke, asked his doctor 'to discontinue all life-supporting services or show me how to do it'. His doctor denied this request, and Hook survived.

Hook's essay, 'In Defense of Voluntary Euthanasia', is the perfect antidote to Randy Pausch: 'Having lived a full and relatively happy life, I would cheerfully accept the chance to be reborn, but certainly not to be reborn again as an infirm octogenarian.' Hook coined the phrase 'mattress graves of pain' to describe the suffering of stroke victims, and concluded his piece with a quotation from the Roman Stoic Seneca: 'the wise man will live as long as he ought, not as long as he can'.

But Hitchens did not adopt Hook's non-interventionist stance. It could be argued that his approach to his cancer treatment was at odds with much that he previously professed to believe (or not believe) in. In *God Is Not Great* he coined the withering phrase 'the tawdriness of the miraculous'. He summarized the views of David Hume approvingly:

A miracle is a disturbance or interruption in the expected and established course of things. This could involve anything from the sun rising in the west to an animal suddenly bursting into the recitation of verse. Very well, then, free will also involves decision. If you seem to witness such a thing, there are two possibilities. The first is that the laws of nature have been suspended (in your favour). The second is that you are under a misapprehension, or suffering from a delusion.

He followed this up with Ambrose Bierce's definition of 'prayer': 'a petition that the laws of nature be suspended in favour of the petitioner; himself confessedly unworthy'. His friends and his doctors might wish to remind themselves of what Hitchens wrote, in good health, in *God Is Not Great*: 'Those who offer false consolation are false friends.' In his memoir, *Hitch-22*, he was scathing of such wishful thinking: 'I try to deny myself any illusions or delusions, and I think that this perhaps entitles me to try and deny the same to others, at least as long as they refuse to keep their fantasies to themselves.'

When Hitchens died at the MD Anderson Cancer Center in Houston, Texas, his wife was clearly not prepared: 'The end was unexpected.' In *Mortality,* she describes how Hitchens, still intubated after a bronchoscopy, and therefore unable to speak, scribbled notes for her, such as: 'I'm staying here [in Houston] until I'm cured. And then I'm taking our families on a vacation to Bermuda.' Interviewed on Australian television after his death, she said:

...it was not clear to his doctors or to us that he was dying. His very radical state-of-the art medical

treatments had proved quite successful and the cancer was in abeyance... the oncologist said he was in
the one per cent of people who would have been
alive then and we hoped that he would either go into
a long remission or certainly have quite a bit more
time. He caught a very, very virulent pneumonia...

Asked by her interviewer whether Hitchens considered
at that time 'it might be the moment to let go?', Blue
answered: 'No, not at all, actually, because he'd been
given such a prognosis. When they did the follow-up scan
basically it was black; no cancer was showing...'

Inevitably, I will be accused of tastelessness in my
analysis of Christopher Hitchens's cancer story. To that
charge, I would say this: Hitchens made a career out of
dissecting the inconsistencies of his opponents' arguments, and might have made similar observations to mine,
had the story been about somebody else. He believed
passionately in the freedom to offend people. We should
be wary, however, of mocking beliefs which we do not
share. One man's delusion and folly is another's 'radical,
childlike hope'. As news of Hitchens's cancer diagnosis
first became widely known, evangelical Christians speculated on the Internet about whether or not his illness
would lead to a religious conversion. In *Mortality*,
Hitchens scoffed at the notion. But in his time of 'living
dyingly', he did find a kind of faith. This was not a return

to the Anglicanism of his upbringing, or the Judaism of his mother's family. Hitchens, the arch-mocker, the debunker of myth, found solace and consolation in the contemporary rites of genetics and oncology.

SUSAN SONTAG:
REFILLING THE POISON CHALICE

Susan Sontag (1933–2004), the American essayist, critic and novelist, did not go gently into that good night. She had – rather miraculously – survived advanced breast cancer in the 1970s, then uterine sarcoma in the 1990s, before finally succumbing to myelodysplastic syndrome (MDS), a type of bone marrow cancer. She had written about sickness in *Illness as Metaphor* and *AIDS and Its Metaphors*. *Swimming in a Sea of Death* (2008), the memoir written by her son David Rieff, begins with the diagnosis of MDS. Sontag and her son visit 'Dr A' in his office to receive the bad news:

> MDS, he explained, slowly and deliberately, as if he had a family of village idiots sitting in front of him, was a particularly lethal form of blood cancer. [I felt for Dr A: 'slowly and deliberately' is how we're taught to impart bad news, regardless of whether the interlocutor is a famous author, or, indeed, a village idiot.]... 'So what you're telling me,' she finally said,

with a poignant deliberation that makes me gasp
even remembering it, 'is that in fact there is nothing
to be done.' After a pause, she added, 'Nothing I can
do.' Dr A did not answer directly, but his silence was,
as the cliché goes, eloquent.

Sontag was not willing to accept this prognosis. After
all, hadn't she confounded her doctors back in the
1970s, when she had advanced breast cancer? She had
initially undergone radical surgery in New York, and
then tracked down a French breast cancer specialist, who
prescribed a novel form of immunotherapy. Whether
this immunotherapy cured Sontag or not is unclear; this
form of treatment did not later go on to become standard
therapy for breast cancer, so it seems unlikely. At any
rate, her astounding good fortune instilled in Sontag an
unshakeable faith in scientific medicine. The experience
also gave her a sense of her own invincibility, a sense
that must have grown stronger when she overcame cancer
for a second time in the 1990s: 'If you were supposed
to die, and you live, in defiance of practically all the
experts' predictions and against all the odds, how can
you not attach some meaning to what has occurred?'
But for all her attachment to science, Sontag had some
flaky Reichian beliefs about the aetiology of cancer: 'I'm
responsible for my cancer. I lived as a coward, repressing
my desire, my rage.'

When she was diagnosed with MDS, Sontag read everything about the condition she could lay her hands on: 'Her apartment became a kind of research unit...' Rieff saw this frantic search for information for what it was: 'magical thinking disguised as practical research'. Although Sontag's book *Illness as Metaphor* had ended with a plea to ditch the military metaphors of the struggle with disease and to 'give such images back to the warmakers', Rieff writes: 'You did not give in to cancer, you fought it, and if you fought hard enough and, above all, intelligently enough, there was a chance that you could win.' Sontag, although uninterested in sport, became obsessed with the cyclist Lance Armstrong. He, more than any famous cancer victim, had championed the concept of 'fighting' it.

This being America, Sontag moved on from the hapless Dr A to the infinitely more encouraging Dr Stephen Nimer at Memorial Sloan-Kettering, the famous New York cancer hospital. Nimer handled the Difficult Conversation with aplomb:

> ...when pressed Stephen Nimer would be very frank
> with my mother about just how terrible her MDS was.
> It is true that he never allowed himself to be drawn
> out on whether he personally thought my mother
> would survive or not (though she repeatedly tried to
> get him to do so, and asked me to ask him on a

number of occasions as well). Instead, he would reframe the question, and in doing so, or so it seemed to me, let the hope back in... it was Nimer himself who determined this outcome. Somehow, whether it was through sheer force of personality, long experience, or psychological acuity, or some combination of all of these, Stephen Nimer managed to make the question 'unaskable' on some deep level.

Nimer referred Sontag to the Fred Hutchinson Cancer Research Center in Seattle, for a bone marrow transplant, despite knowing – as he must have done – that the chances of success were very slim: 'And they were going ahead with treatment, presumably in the belief that it was not futile, and that she was not wrong to hope.' Rieff quotes a brochure on MDS, which suggests that his mother was not suitable for this treatment: 'In the very small proportion of patients who are under 50 years of age with a severe form of myelodysplastic syndrome, intensive radiation and/or chemotherapy followed by allogenic stem cell transplantation can be considered.' Sontag was seventy-one, and not, by any objective criterion, a good candidate for this treatment. Nimer (as quoted by Rieff) clearly believed that it was worth trying, even if the likelihood of a cure was remote: 'Susan told me from the outset that she wanted me to do everything she could to save her life, and so we could go straight into a discussion about *what she wanted* [my italics] and what the plan would be.' After the publication of Rieff's memoir, it emerged that Sontag's medical insurance had refused to pay for the transplant, and that she had to pay a deposit of $250,000 on admission to the Seattle hospital.

When she arrived at the Fred Hutchinson Cancer Research Center, 'its clinical research director, Fred Appelbaum, dropped by to remind my mother of the poor survival statistics... she was devastated. That evening, still completely devastated, she kept repeating, "Why would he tell me such a thing?"' Rieff gives us the simple answer: 'I remembered having read somewhere that the Hutch had been taken to court, accused by the relatives of some patients whose loved ones had not survived their transplants of not having warned them of how small their chances of survival had really been.' In that single sentence, we have the double-bind of modern oncology: if the doctor does not carry out the futile treatment, he is heartless and has condemned his patient to hopelessness and death; if he does carry out the treatment, the surviving relatives will sue him for failing to be realistic with the Loved One. In fact, it's a triple bind: if he does carry out the futile treatment, and he is realistic with the patient, she is 'devastated'.

The transplant inevitably failed; when told, Sontag screamed: 'But this means I'm going to die!' She went back to New York to the relentlessly upbeat Dr Nimer. Rieff, who clearly detested Dr A ('I prefer not to name him'), whom he describes as fat, overbearing and patronizing, positively hero-worships Nimer: 'But for Nimer, the essence of being a doctor was doing everything possible for his patients, even if it meant trying experimental therapies where the chances of success were not high.'

Sontag's condition steadily deteriorated, but she refused to accept that she was dying, and her son felt unable to be frank with her: 'What conversations I had with her about her prognosis soon became almost lawyerly exercises.' Sontag had what I would call a 'wild' death: 'there was nothing easy about my mother's death, except, literally, her last few hours. It was hard, and it was slow – sometimes the days of her dying seemed to me actually to be taking place in slow motion – and in the process it was not only my mother who was stripped of her dignity.'

Rieff felt keenly and bitterly his failure to engage with his mother and the fact of her dying: 'I am anything but certain that I did the right thing, and in my bleaker moments, wonder if in fact I might not have made things worse for her by endlessly refilling that poisoned chalice of hope.' I think he is hard on himself – he never had a chance. Sontag herself steadfastly refused to even contemplate her mortality. At one point, after yet another delusional talk with his mother about all the things she would do after the bone marrow transplant cured her, Rieff finally collapsed: 'I finally broke down, I wept. But my stupefaction was almost as great as my grief. I kept thinking, "she really does not know what is happening to her. She still believes that she is going to survive."' After Sontag's death, Nimer contacted Rieff by email, almost in the guise of a grieving relative: 'I think about Susan all the time. We have to do better.' Although Rieff finally begins to harbour some niggling doubts, nothing can shake his faith in Nimer as a 'great doctor', such is the force of Nimer's personality, more 'physician-shaman' than 'physician-scientist'. I wonder how Sean O'Mahony would have handled Susan Sontag.

Rieff buried his mother in Montparnasse, in Paris. In 2006, two years after Sontag's death, her former lover, the photographer Annie Leibovitz, put on an exhibition of her work over the previous fifteen years at the Brooklyn Museum. The collection included two photographs of Sontag: one taken when she was in Seattle for her transplant, where she looks bloated and clearly very ill, the second after her death, taken in a back room of the Frank E. Campbell Funeral Chapel in New York. Rieff was appalled, and called the photographs 'carnival images of celebrity death'.

JOSEPHINE HART:
'MEDIEVAL, DEGRADING AND INEFFECTIVE'

Josephine Hart (1942–2011) began life in the distinctly unglamorous environs of Mullingar, County Westmeath. She had a traumatic childhood: by the time she was seventeen, three of her siblings were dead. She moved to London, toyed with acting, and ended up in magazine publishing. A first marriage ended in divorce, but in her second, to advertising multi-millionaire and Tory peer Maurice Saatchi, she had found her soulmate. Her first novel, *Damage* (1991) was a bestseller and was adapted into a successful film. She organized fashionable poetry readings with recitations by famous actors, produced plays, and was a prominent figure on the London literary scene. She enjoyed the lifestyle that came with her second marriage. In person, she came across as intense and a little scary.

In 2010, Hart was diagnosed with a rare type of pelvic cancer, primary peritoneal carcinoma. She died in 2011. Her husband has spoken frequently and eloquently of his grief, and has gone into semi-permanent mourning. He visits his wife's grave every day, where he eats his breakfast and talks to her. Geoffrey Gorer would have approved. Saatchi has described her cancer treatment as 'medieval, degrading and ineffective'. Clearly not used to being thwarted, Saatchi has declared his own war on cancer. (A previous declaration of war on cancer by Richard Nixon was not notably successful.) Saatchi proposed a private member's Bill, the Medical Innovation Bill, in the House of Lords in 2013, with the intention of giving doctors the freedom to treat cancer patients with 'cutting-edge' and 'revolutionary' treatments, without the fear of litigation. Clearly, Saatchi has been motivated by witnessing the horrors of his wife's illness and death, but I detect also a whiff of pique: before his wife's cancer, I imagine that he solved most problems with his money and influence. He was interviewed in 2013 by Elizabeth Grice of the *Daily Telegraph*:

> In desperation, Saatchi trawled the Internet for news of hopeful discoveries. The future of cancer science seemed to lie in mapping the cancer genome and providing less toxic therapies. 'Why couldn't Josephine Hart have the future of science?' He approached Harvard Medical School with details of her case. They analysed his wife's tumour and sent back a thick report with a covering letter that said: 'The good news is that your wife's tumour is non-mutational.' Her own doctors were unimpressed. 'Isn't this genetic profiling very important?' Saatchi asked. He was told: 'It's irrelevant.' That was the tipping point; the moment he knew he would eventually have to challenge the adherence to standard practice.

The man who once ran the biggest advertising agency in the world, who is credited with helping bring Margaret Thatcher to power in 1979, made his intentions clear: 'I intend to cure cancer, you see. I mean to do it. I expect to do it.' Saatchi was not previously very exercised about cancer: Silk Cut (a brand of cigarette) was one of Saatchi & Saatchi's biggest accounts.

It is not clear to me how this change in legislation would 'cure' cancer. Although Saatchi's PR campaign was slick and influential, informed opinion, including the Royal Colleges (Physicians, Surgeons and General Practitioners) and the British Medical Association, saw no need for such legislation. More than one hundred oncologists wrote to *The Times* opposing the Medical Innovation Bill: 'We are concerned that rather than promoting responsible scientific innovation in the treatment of cancer, the Medical Innovation Bill will actually encourage irresponsible experimentation producing nothing more than anecdotal "evidence", at the potential expense of causing serious harm and suffering to patients.' Saatchi was furious, and raged in the *Guardian*: 'The 100 doctors who wrote to *The Times* rubbishing my medical innovation bill are the authentic voice of complacency... How I pity their patients.' In January 2015, the influential cancer journal *The Lancet Oncology* devoted an editorial to the Bill. In it, Saatchi's personal credentials ('an unelected individual with no professional medical or scientific training') were loftily dismissed, and the authors went on to explain that doctors are already able to innovate outside clinical trials: 'There are many ways in which doctors can access drugs that are in early-stage clinical trials but not yet widely available. However, provision of these agents on a desperate whim, in an unmonitored environment, could lead to patient harm.' The Bill, concluded the editorial, 'strikes at the heart of evidence-based medicine'.

Although Saatchi threw his considerable PR talents and financial resources into drumming up support for his Bill, it was doomed. One of the last decisions taken by Norman Lamb, junior Health Minister in the Conservative/Liberal Democrat coalition government, was to veto it in the House of Commons.

The story of the Medical Innovation Bill is an interesting one. Many people bereaved by cancer feel an understandable desire to find some meaning in their loss. Maurice Saatchi's wish to honour the memory of his wife is admirable, and this desire for something good to emerge from a cancer death is a common emotion among the bereaved. Relatives often set up voluntary groups to fundraise for research, or to provide new facilities. Few such relatives, however, have Maurice Saatchi's influence and wealth. His *idée fixe* was indulged by many journalists and politicians, a troubling reflection of a woeful ignorance of science. The main beneficiaries of such legislation would have been quacks and the pharmaceutical industry.

The notion that we are all scientific experts is a threat to freedom: if we are not careful, the rich and media-savvy will become our law-makers. Maurice Saatchi's grief is, in its own way, noble, but his grief will not cure cancer.

NUALA O'FAOLAIN:
'MY DESPAIR IS MY OWN'

The late Nuala O'Faolain (1940–2008) sparked a national debate in Ireland about death and dying in April 2008, when she was interviewed on radio by her old friend, the broadcaster Marian Finucane. I confess I was never a fan of O'Faolain's. Her upbringing in Dublin was spectacularly dysfunctional. Having worked as a journalist and television producer for many years, she wrote, in her fifties, a bestselling memoir *Are You Somebody?* (1996). She left her long-time lover, the journalist and feminist Nell McCafferty, and moved to New York, where she began a relationship with a lawyer, John Low-Beer.

In February 2008 she noticed a weakness in her arm and went to the emergency room of her local hospital in New York. After a series of scans, she was told that she had tumours in her brain, lung and liver, with the likely primary being in her lung. O'Faolain had been a heavy smoker, but had quit ten years before. She declined chemotherapy, but agreed to some palliative radiation treatment for the brain tumours. She returned to Ireland to die. The interview was a national sensation: the Irish, so good with the dead, are not so good around the dying.

O'Faolain was stark and brutally honest; she made no attempt to put a positive spin on her situation. It seemed that the country stopped whatever it was doing to listen. The Irish were not used to such candour about the subject of death. Here was a situation that could not be mollified or shrugged away. You won't, in the stock Irish phrase, be 'grand'; there is no hope:

> I was just reading about some best-selling man who says 'Live your dream to the end' and so on and I don't despise anyone who does, but I don't see it that way. Even if I gained time through the chemotherapy, it isn't time I want. Because as soon as I knew I was going to die soon, the goodness went out of life... I'm not nice or anything – I'm not getting nicer. I'm sour and difficult, you know. I don't know how my friends and family are putting up with me, but they are, heroically...
>
> ...I think there's a wonderful rule of life that means that we do not consider our own mortality. I know we seem to, and remember, 'man, thou art but dust', but I don't believe we do. I believe there's an absolute difference between knowing you are likely

to die, let's say within the next year, and not knowing
when you are going to die – an absolute difference...

Marian Finucane began to get a little alarmed by the
tone of the interview: 'If there are people who have
cancer or loved ones who have cancer and passionately
believe that the treatments are going to work for them,
there is a possibility that this could cast a despair over
them.' O'Faolain replied imperiously: 'My despair is
my own, their hope is their own... My way of looking at
the world is my own. We each end up differently facing
this common fate. I wish everybody out there a miracle
cure... I thought there would be me and the world, but
the world turned its back on me.'

O'Faolain was shocking, not just for her honesty, but
for her rebellion against the notions that cancer must
be 'battled' to the bitter end, and that dying should be,
in some way, a phase of personal growth, a 'spiritual'
experience. She was genuinely surprised by the response
to the interview, which was overwhelmingly one of good-
will, and offers of help. O'Faolain later remarked that she
had not realized there was so much goodness in people.
She had mentioned in the interview how she had left new,
expensive curtains in New York which she would never get
to use: several listeners offered to go to her apartment and
bring them back to Ireland. A neighbour cleaned out her
house and put down a fire. O'Faolain was so overwhelmed

that she planned to do a second interview, 'to redress the balance', but she died soon after. Shortly before her death, she visited Berlin with her friend, the writer Hugo Hamilton. He wrote a lightly fictionalised account of this trip called *Every Single Minute.*

Of all these stories, O'Faolain's is the one that is most true. Her vivid acceptance of *how it is* is bracing. Her despair is her own – death is only affliction. Unlike Hitchens and Sontag, she rejected the bright hopes offered by oncology. Like Sontag, she raged against death and refused to give us childish bromides about the spirituality of dying. Unlike Sontag, she confronted and acknowledged her mortality. I have come to admire her.

ONCOLOGY, SCHMONCOLOGY

I am, I confess, an oncology apostate. Cancer treatment seems to offer some patients a toxic combination of false hopes and a bad death. Even those within oncology, or the 'cancer community' as they sometimes call themselves, accept that the current model of cancer care in developed countries has now become unaffordable and unsustainable. The Lancet Oncology Commission (not exactly a cranky fringe group, but a gathering of the great and the good of modern oncology) produced a lengthy report in 2011, a few months before Christopher Hitchens died, called 'Delivering Affordable Cancer Care in High-income Countries'. The Commission concluded that cancer care is in crisis, driven by over-use and futility, and that 'the medical profession and the health-care industry have created unrealistic expectations of arrest of disease and death. This set of expectations allows inappropriate application of relatively ineffective therapies, including surgery, in the name of care. In developed countries, cancer treatment is becoming a culture of excess.' The American Society of Clinical Oncology found that as many as 10 to 15 per cent of patients with cancer receive chemotherapy in the last two weeks of life. Much cancer treatment – particularly chemotherapy – is given for no better reason than the need to be seen to 'do something'. A good deal of therapeutics is founded on the naïve assumption that there is a treatment for every ill. The physician and writer Richard Asher glumly admitted that 'it is better to believe in therapeutic nonsense, than to openly admit to therapeutic bankruptcy'. As a placebo and a ritual, chemotherapy comes at a high price.

Any attempt at reasoned debate is trumped by the emotive examples of individuals with cancer. In 2012, the Irish Health Service decided not to fund treatment of advanced melanoma (skin cancer) with a new, very expensive drug called ipilimumab. A distinguished professor of pharmacology & therapeutics went on national radio to explain that this drug benefited a small minority of patients, at an exorbitant cost (€85,000 per patient), and that he therefore could not recommend its funding by the Irish government. Days later, a woman with advanced melanoma was also interviewed on national radio. The story was heartbreaking: this woman, aged forty-one, had three young children; her oncologist had advised her that this new drug was her only hope. The next day, on the instruction of the Minster for Health, the Irish Health Service Executive reversed its decision on ipilimumab and agreed to fund treatment for sixty patients, including this woman. She died three months later.

One of the root causes of this crisis in cancer care is sentimentality. I am often told by well-meaning family members that their stricken relative is a 'fighter', by which they mean that the known biological statistics appropriate to other, lesser souls, do not apply in this particular case. Lance Armstrong persuaded many cancer sufferers, including the singularly unsporty Susan Sontag, that cancer could be 'beaten' by sheer force of will. This kind of sentimentality is at the root of Maurice Saatchi's impotent rage against the disease that took his wife's life.

The American science writer George Johnson observed of this sentimentality in *The Cancer Chronicles* (2013): 'Now there is a cancer culture, and whether you had a harmless in-situ carcinoma removed with a simple lumpectomy or are fighting the terminal stages of metastatic melanoma, you are called a survivor. In the first case there was nothing to survive. In the second case there will be no survival.' The Irish Cancer Society has launched an 'ambitious new strategy statement' for 2013 to 2017 entitled *Towards a Future without Cancer*. They modestly concede that 'this may not be achieved in the lifetime of this strategy statement'. Cancer Research UK's current campaign proclaims: 'We *will* beat cancer.'

CRACKING THE CODE

As far back as 1993, Christopher Hitchens wrote about biogenetics in *Vanity Fair*: 'One need not be Utopian about biogenetics, which like any other breakthrough can be exploited by the unscrupulous.' When I was a junior research doctor in the late 1980s, my colleagues used to joke that inclusion of the phrase 'genetic polymorphism' in the title was enough to get any scientific paper published. Since the 1980s, molecular biology/genetics has been the dominant force in laboratory medicine and has been lavishly funded by government agencies. There is now, however, a grudging acceptance in the scientific and medical communities that, despite all the advances in genetics, including the sequencing of the entire human genome, there have been precious few applications for treatment of cancer and other serious diseases.

In 2000, Bill Clinton announced the completion of the £3 billion Human Genome Project. Francis Collins, then head of the National Human Genome Research Institute, predicted that a new era of 'personalized medicine' would emerge by 2010: genetic tests would routinely identify an individual's risk for various common diseases. Genetics would provide powerful new treatments for cancer and guide treatment in individual cases. This, as we know, and as Christopher Hitchens and Maurice Saatchi discovered, hasn't happened. The returns on cancer genomics have been very modest indeed, considering the investment. Although basic science has benefited from the Human Genome Project, cancer treatment has seen relatively few improvements.

Steve Jones, Emeritus Professor of Genetics at University College London, admitted as much in 2009, when he wrote: 'We thought it [genetic research] was going to change our lives but that has turned out to be a false dawn.' He went on to suggest that too much money had been spent on genetic research, and that such scarce funding would be better used elsewhere. Many took issue with Jones's nihilism, but most agreed that genetics has not led to the advances that had been hoped for.

Cancer is a privileged disease. If there is a bed crisis at my hospital, all 'non-cancer' elective activity is commonly cancelled. Only cancer is immune to the quotidian realities of an over-stretched, state-funded medical system. I worked in the NHS when the 'two-week cancer rule' was introduced: any patient with suspected cancer had to be seen at a specialist clinic within two weeks. The definition of 'suspected cancer' was highly nebulous and included indigestion in anyone over the age of fifty. Overnight, an entire new bureaucracy sprung up to deal with this diktat. Non-cancer doctors have watched and learned, and as specialties have to compete with each other for finite resources, the phenomenon of 'my disease is better than your disease' has emerged. My younger colleagues now regard public relations as part of their job. Every disease has a patient support group (frequently funded by pharmaceutical companies), and specialist medical societies employ marketing and PR advisers. Cystic fibrosis is the perfect example of 'my disease is better than your disease': the victims are young and the condition is not self-induced. The other 'good' diseases are breast cancer and anything affecting children. My particular end of the medical swamp is unfashionable and under-funded. Alcoholic liver disease doesn't induce much public sympathy; we don't have a celebrity liver cirrhosis sufferer to lead a campaign.

The stories of Christopher Hitchens and Susan Sontag tell us much about the reality of dying from cancer. Both of them were enthusiastic believers in modern scientific oncology and especially in the personal powers of their oncologists. Would Maurice Saatchi have been more reconciled to his wife's death, I wonder, had Stephen Nimer been her oncologist?

STEPHEN JAY GOULD:
THE MEDIAN IS NOT THE MESSAGE

It is not my intention to mock Hitchens and Sontag; what might be right for mankind, or society, is rarely what is right for me. Christopher Hitchens abandoned his lifelong and celebrated scepticism when faced with cancer. Were I to be faced with a diagnosis of stage IV oesophageal cancer, or MDS, I do not know how I would react, particularly if I were treated by an oncologist with such a powerful personality as Stephen Nimer. I might be inspired by the story of Stephen Jay Gould, the palaeontologist and writer. In 1982, Gould was diagnosed with the rare cancer, primary peritoneal mesothelioma. (Mesothelioma, as in Kieran Sweeney's case, usually affects the lung.) Gould, being a scientist, examined the statistics and literature on this cancer and found to his horror that the median survival was eight months – that is, 50 per cent of patients were dead at eight months after diagnosis. Gould wrote a famous essay, 'The Median Isn't the Message' (1985):

When I learned about the eight-month median, my

first intellectual reaction was: fine, half the people will live longer; now what are my chances of being in that half. I read for a furious and nervous hour and concluded, with relief: damned good. I possessed every one of the characteristics conferring a probability of longer life: I was young; my disease had been recognized in a relatively early stage; I would receive the nation's best medical treatment; I had the world to live for; I knew how to read the data properly and not despair.

Gould noticed, too, that the survival 'bell-curve' was not symmetrical, that it was 'right-skewed', with a small minority of long-term survivors:

> I saw no reason why I shouldn't be in that small tail, and I breathed a very long sigh of relief. My technical knowledge had helped. I had read the graph correctly. I had asked the right question and found the answers. I had obtained, in all probability, the most precious of all possible gifts in the circumstances – substantial time.

Gould survived for another twenty years, dying of an unrelated cancer. The vast majority of patients with cancer are not so lucky, but our medical system is based around the assumption that everyone with cancer might, just might, be 'in that small tail' of long-term survivors. Treatment is aimed at that tiny minority, not the great majority, who are not as fortunate as Stephen Jay Gould. And yet, and yet... Gould argued: 'It has become, in my view, a bit too trendy to regard the acceptance of death as something tantamount to intrinsic dignity... I prefer the more martial view that death is the ultimate enemy – and I find nothing reproachable in those who rage mightily against the dying of the light.'

The Battle against Cancer is often described in military terms; Atul Gawande uses a military analogy of a different kind to describe the treatment of patients with incurable cancer:

> And in a war that you cannot win, you don't want a general who fights to the point of total annihilation. You don't want Custer, you want Robert E. Lee, someone who knows how to fight for territory that can be won and how to surrender when it can't, someone who understands that the damage is greatest if all you do is battle to the bitter end.

Oncology, unfortunately, has more Custers than Lees.

An acquaintance of mine was diagnosed with lung cancer in his fifties. He underwent surgery and was well for about four years. But the cancer returned and he was found to have multiple secondary deposits in his bones. He was sent to the oncologist, who told him: 'We can treat this.' Technically true, but what the oncologist meant was: 'We can give chemotherapy for this, but it won't cure you.' His patient heard: 'We can cure this.' This is also what his wife and adult children heard. His condition gradually worsened until he was unable to work, or even get up from the chair. His wife (with whom he had a difficult relationship) even suspected that he was somehow malingering. Then, as so often happens, he had a sudden, acute deterioration. The oncologist admitted there was nothing more she could do and advised admission to the local hospice, where he died a few days later. My point is this: had the oncologist had the courage to be more honest, he and his family might have had a more realistic expectation of the future. True, the man might still have opted for chemotherapy, but would have been aware of its likely modest benefit. His family might have been more supportive. He might have had the opportunity to settle his affairs and be reconciled with his wife.

There is a schism within medicine. Palliative care is trying to return to tame death – or at least a modern variant of it, while oncology is pulling patients in a different direction. Oncology, for all its claims to being at the cutting edge of medical science, has more than a touch of primitive shamanic ritual about it.

CHAPTER 7

A Passion for Control

The West has ideas about dying which are dominated by individualism, and this individualism, in turn, has influenced both the development of the hospice movement and the modern clamour for assisted suicide. The two great contemporary debates about dying – assisted suicide and advance directives, or living wills – are both informed by a passion for personal autonomy: for control.

LET ME DIE

The idea of the advance directive is superficially attractive. At the end of life, modern medical care is often unthinking and futile. Families and doctors sometimes collude – with the best of intentions – in subjecting those with no hope of recovery to painful, prolonged and ineffective treatments. The default setting of modern medicine is full intervention, unless you are instructed otherwise. Families and patients, moreover, may lack the necessary education and medical knowledge to make truly informed decisions. Very often, for example, when trying to nudge a family towards minimal intervention in the case of an acutely ill, very old person, I am told: 'Just do everything you can, Doc.'

Frail old folk are commonly sent from nursing homes to Emergency Departments, where it is not unknown for them to die alone, on a trolley, in a busy corridor. For all sorts of reasons, administrative and legal, it is easier (for the nursing home and referring doctor) if these people die in hospital. Picture the scene: it is the Saturday evening of a Bank Holiday weekend, and a resident of a nursing home becomes acutely unwell. She is eighty-eight years old, has advanced dementia, and a number of other medical problems, including emphysema, angina, diabetes and leg ulcers. She has become more confused than usual, and has stopped eating and drinking. She has developed a fever and is a bit short of breath. The nurse on duty at the home calls the doctor, who is a locum employed by the out-of-hours deputizing service run by the local GP cooperative, not the patient's usual doctor.

The locum has never seen this patient before. The doctor examines the old woman and diagnoses a chest infection. Treating her with oral antibiotics in the nursing home is a potentially dangerous strategy: what if she deteriorates, or even dies? What if the family complain that not enough was done? Much safer to call for an ambulance and send the patient to the Emergency Department, where she becomes somebody else's responsibility. In my hospital, during a single month in 2015, eleven patients transferred from nursing homes died within thirty minutes of arrival at the Emergency Department.

So our patient arrives at the hospital, and is wheeled past the drunks in the waiting room of the Emergency Department. All the cubicles are full, so she is left in the corridor. She is upset and frightened by this strange environment. After a long wait, during which she grows ever more bewildered and disorientated, she is seen and examined by a junior doctor. A chest X-ray shows pneumonia, and her blood oxygen levels are low, so she is moved to the resuscitation room, where she is given intravenous antibiotics and oxygen. Her condition gets worse during the night and the medical registrar contacts (with some difficulty) her family. The woman's son eventually arrives at the hospital; he has not seen his mother for several weeks. The registrar patiently tells the son that his mother's condition is deteriorating. She tries to explain that, in her view, more intensive treatment, such as mechanical ventilation (with a breathing machine) in intensive care would not be appropriate for his mother. The son finds it difficult to understand what is being said to him, but eventually agrees to be guided by the doctor. The woman's condition steadily worsens, and the medical registrar pronounces her dead in the resuscitation room, at 5.00 a.m. The coroner is duly informed, a legal requirement when a nursing home resident dies.

The sequence of events I describe is not an uncommon one. Some cases are messier – for example, when the family demands intensive intervention against the advice of the doctors. Can we conceive of a better alternative for this lady? Well, yes, we can: a frail, demented woman with multiple serious medical problems would probably be best treated in the nursing home if she develops an acute illness such as pneumonia. True, she may possibly die of this pneumonia, but she will die in the environment that she has become comfortable with, and attended by the people who have cared for her. Many factors currently conspire against this: nursing homes are increasingly fearful of being accused of neglect; outside of routine office hours, a sick nursing-home resident is likely to be seen by a doctor who is unfamiliar with them; families – even those of elderly demented people – sometimes harbour unrealistic expectations of medical care.

One potential solution is to introduce advance

directives for such patients. Willie Molloy, Professor of Geriatrics at University College Cork, is a leader in this field and has started a pilot programme of advance directives for nursing home residents in Cork. This programme is called 'Let Me Decide' and is quite complex. It starts with a Mini-Mental State Examination (MMSE), which yields a score that gives a reasonably good indication of whether or not the patient has dementia. A second score, the 'Screening Instrument to Assess Capacity to complete an Advance Directive' (SIACAD) is then calculated. If the person has dementia or lacks the capacity to fill in the form, a proxy is nominated. The patient (or the proxy) is offered a menu of options: so, for life-threatening illness, they can choose between four different levels of care: palliative, limited, surgical or intensive. In the event of a cardiac arrest, there are two choices: cardio-pulmonary resuscitation or not. In the event of feeding difficulties, there are two choices: 'basic' or 'tube'. Several signatures (the patient, the proxy, the GP and the witness) are required.

A couple of years ago, I attended a lecture on advance directives. The speaker used several hypothetical clinical scenarios to illustrate his argument, and to provoke reaction from the audience. One of these was the case of a frail elderly man sent in from a nursing home with bleeding from his stomach. The usual initial approach to this problem is to carry out an endoscopy to diagnose the cause of bleeding (usually an ulcer); very often, the bleeding can be stopped by injecting or clipping the ulcer. This treatment is remarkably effective in many cases, and usually takes no longer than ten to fifteen minutes. It is nearly always performed under mild sedation, and I have carried out this procedure on many very old people with 'multiple co-morbidity' (several other diseases). On the Let Me Decide menu, however, this intervention would be classified as 'surgical'. Had this old man's treatment been guided by an advance directive – assuming he had decided against 'surgical' intervention – he would have been denied a simple, usually safe and potentially life-saving treatment. How could a lay person possibly know all this?

Advance directives provide endless potential opportunity for conflict. Siblings and spouses will quarrel over who should have the power of proxy; patients may challenge an assessment that concludes that they lack capacity. Large acute hospitals may need to employ lawyers to deal specifically with these documents. Hospital staff may waste valuable time trying to locate the document when the patient is admitted as an emergency case. Busy on-call staff may not bother to ascertain whether or not the patient has an advance directive, and proceed to treat them regardless. Relatives may put pressure on medical staff to override the document (this is a common occurrence in the US where advance directives have been legal for many years). In acute medicine, where there is doubt, doctors generally opt for full, invasive treatment. You can argue later.

My first experience of an advance directive document was not encouraging. An elderly man, a nursing home resident with dementia and a number of other medical problems, came under my care suffering from pneumonia and heart failure. His condition was not initially worrying, but during the night he became progressively more unwell, and was moved from the main emergency area into the resuscitation room. I went to see him, and decided that we needed to make a decision quickly about how far we should go with treatment. If his condition got any worse, we would have to decide if he should be admitted to the Intensive Care Unit. I spoke with the man and asked him who his nearest relative was; he told me he didn't have any immediate family and that his next-of-kin was a nephew. I phoned the nephew, who told me that his uncle had filled out a 'living will' at the nursing home. I searched in vain in his notes and referral letter for the advance directive; the nursing home hadn't bothered to send it with him to the Emergency Department. I eventually obtained a faxed copy of the document, which clearly specified that this man did not wish to have cardio-pulmonary resuscitation (CPR), and thus, by extrapolation, admission to the Intensive Care Unit. I discussed the matter with my team: we concluded that had the man suffered a cardiac arrest in the night, he would have undergone cardio-pulmonary resuscitation; had this been successful – which was, admittedly, unlikely – he would have woken up in the Intensive Care Unit, intubated.

Advance directives will only encourage the creeping 'lawyerization' of medical practice. But my main concern with advance directives is this: in your health, and in your still vigorous middle age, or early old age, you might quite rightly regard, let us say, a devastating middle-cerebral artery stroke as a condition not worth living with – assuming, of course, that you know what a 'devastating middle-cerebral artery stroke' is. And the same goes for dementia, or motor neurone disease. The trouble is, you don't know how you will react until that awful event occurs. You may well wish to cling onto life, no matter how diminished its quality. You may very well accept a life that in the fullness of your health you would have rejected as not worth living. The instinct to live is profoundly powerful, and in our health and vigour we underestimate it.

Let us take the example of locked-in syndrome, a type of brain-stem stroke which leaves the victim's mind intact but deprived of nearly all bodily movement except, perhaps, for a flicker of the eye. They are literally locked in their own bodies. The condition became well known mainly because of Jean-Dominique Bauby's account of the affliction, *The Diving-Bell and the Butterfly* (1997). Tony Nicklinson, who had the syndrome, campaigned for the right to have his life ended. Richard Ford was a fit, forty-one-year-old policeman based in Leeds when he was struck down with the same disorder. Nicklinson has since died (without any assistance), but Richard Ford clearly wants to live. He told the *Sunday Times Magazine*: 'People think they can't stand this, but you can and you do. People believe in me. I am determined not to let them or myself down. I have a lot to live for, a lot to look forward to. A lot of memories to make.' He spoke to the journalist 'with excruciating deliberation', using his eye-gaze computer. And Richard Ford is not alone. A survey of French patients with locked-in syndrome showed that a majority who were interviewed reported a good quality of life. Richard Ford concluded with Yorkshire matter-of-factness: 'The most important thing is you're heard, your opinion still counts and you're entitled to change your mind. I never wanted this and I might just prove everybody wrong, but I've never stopped wanting to go on living.' What was 'dull, miserable, demeaning, undignified and intolerable' for Tony Nicklinson is not so for Richard Ford.

Explaining sometimes complex medical/technological issues to patients and families is often an insurmountable problem. 'Informed consent' is a legalistic fantasy, which works only for the truly 'informed', that is, educated, middle-class people with biomedical knowledge. We have fetishized 'choice', but choice, for many people, is bewildering. Medicine is now so complex that many, if not most, elderly people cannot possibly understand the various treatment options. These forms, like many such documents, tend to be written by committees, far from the realities and uncertainties of clinical medicine. Can we make this any easier? In the US, advance directives have been part of the medical landscape for many years, so doctors there have had some time to work on these issues. Angelo Volandes, a physician at the Massachusetts General Hospital in Boston founded Advance Care Planning (ACP) Decisions to assist dying patients to choose the care they want. Volandes has made simple videos, free of medical jargon, which explain the types of care available to dying patients. These videos are short and can be watched on a laptop or iPad. Volandes spoke to the *Sunday Times*:

Patients don't understand what they might be in for. They've seen CPR (Cardio-Pulmonary Resuscitation) on *ER* and think it always works. In real life it usually doesn't result in miraculous recovery but guarantees a violent death... Of course people are right to be worried about a doctor pulling the plug on grandma, but it's a very different issue when it's grandma saying, 'don't put the plug in'.

But it's not as simple as Dr Volandes suggests. It is interesting, and instructive, to read about the US experience. Doctors there – usually in collusion with families – commonly ignore advance directives. Very often, the slow course of a long illness makes it difficult to know when to invoke the provisions of the directive. When there is any uncertainty, doctors and families generally opt for full intervention.

Intriguingly, decisions about end-of-life care may be influenced by the way the options are presented, or 'framed'. Using ideas well known to behavioural economists, Dr Scott Halpern of the University of Pennsylvania showed that the 'default setting' of advance directive documents strongly influenced patients' choices. If the default setting was 'comfort', patients were more likely to opt for this, whereas if the default setting was full CPR, more chose this. Changing the language from 'do not resuscitate' to 'allow a natural death' also changed patients' choices. Halpern calls this 'nudging'. If I were to choose one core skill for doctors treating the dying and their families, it would be the ability to 'nudge' people to make choices that will best help them.

Americans appear to be ambivalent about advance directives. In 2009, when President Obama's Affordable Care Act proposed that doctors should be paid for having a discussion about end-of-life care with their patients, Sarah Palin and others claimed that this would introduce 'death panels'. Although the accusation was absurd, the proposal was dropped.

Advance directives perpetuate an illusion that we can control, in minute detail, our treatment of an unpredictable illness at some unknown time in the future. This ignores the contingent nature of life and death. Nevertheless, many doctors, including Atul Gawande, are enthusiastic supporters of advance directives. They point to the studies which show that employment of these directives dramatically reduces admission of nursing-home patients to acute hospitals at the end of life. Enthusiasm for advance directives, along with the campaign for assisted suicide, is fuelled by the perception that old people need protection from modern medicine. Even if this is only partly true, it should be a cause of collective shame. We have, as a profession, come to a pretty pass when our patients stop trusting their doctors, and see us as an obstacle to a peaceful death. Perhaps we will have to accept advance directives as a necessary evil, and an admission of our failure to treat the elderly and the dying with compassion and common sense.

DON'T LET ME DIE

The success rate of cardio-pulmonary resuscitation (defined as the resumption of a spontaneous circulation) is 18 per cent; the perception of the general public is that it is closer to 50 per cent. This perception may be due to television: a study published in the *New England Journal of Medicine* in 1996 analysed the depiction of CPR in two popular medical television dramas – *ER* and *Chicago Hope*, and one 'reality-based' show, *Rescue 911*. In the 60 occurrences of CPR in 97 television episodes, 75 per cent of the 'patients' were successfully resuscitated.

In the 82 per cent in whom CPR is unsuccessful, death is preceded by a period – usually lasting about twenty minutes – of 'bagging' (filling the lungs with air via an endotracheal tube using a manually powered 'bag') and cardiac massage. Drugs such as adrenaline are injected, sometimes directly into the heart, with a long needle (rather like the one John Travolta uses to revive Uma Thurman in *Pulp Fiction*). Rib fractures are very common. Doctors do the bagging and cardiac massage in relays. The most senior member of the arrest team eventually calls 'time'. Remember that most of these resuscitation attempts take place in general wards, in close proximity to other patients, who will hear everything from the other side of the curtain. Thankfully, most people dying in hospital don't undergo CPR, but 20 per cent do: so, for one in five people, their last experience on this earth is bloody, violent and futile.

In those 18 per cent in whom CPR is successful, the vast majority spend a prolonged period in intensive care. Many are left with permanent brain damage. I recall the case of the father of a school friend. He had a cardiac arrest at his workplace. The ambulance crew managed to resuscitate him, and he was admitted to the Intensive Care Unit. When he woke up, he was raving. And he stayed raving for the remaining two years of his life.

Twenty years ago, a distant relative of mine, a man in his late sixties, had a coronary angiogram; the purpose of this procedure is to obtain X-rays of the coronary arteries, and it is commonly performed as part of the work-up for bypass surgery. The cardiologist performing the procedure gains access to the vascular system by puncturing the femoral artery in the groin, and through that a catheter is advanced up to the heart. The puncture in my relative's femoral artery bled profusely the night after the procedure. He bled so much that his heart stopped beating and his brain was deprived of oxygen for many minutes. He was 'successfully' resuscitated, and the puncture was repaired. When he woke, he was raving. He survived for another twelve years, raving.

One of our hospital chaplains told me how he was called to give the last rites to a ninety-five-year-old man brought to the emergency room by ambulance. He had dementia, and was a resident of a nursing home twenty miles away. He had become acutely unwell in the nursing home; when he stopped breathing in the ambulance, the paramedics administered CPR, because they were afraid not to. He arrived at the emergency room, a bruised corpse.

Janet Tracey and her family might have saved them-selves, their doctors and the English legal system a lot of grief had they watched Dr Volandes's video on CPR. In 2011, Mrs Tracey, aged sixty-three, was diagnosed with advanced and incurable lung cancer. Two weeks later, on 19 February 2011, she was involved in a road traffic accident and sustained serious injuries, including a broken neck. She was taken to Addenbrooke's Hospital in Cambridge, where she was admitted to the ICU. In a 2014 paper published in the journal *Clinical Medicine*, Zoë Fritz et al. summarized the subsequent events:

> She had metastatic lung cancer and chronic lung disease with an estimated prognosis of 9 months. She was intubated and ventilated, and had two failed extubations. The family were informed that, if the third extubation failed, Mrs Tracey would be 'allowed to slip away', but there was no documenta-tion of a discussion with Mrs Tracey.
>
> A DNACPR form was written, and Mrs Tracey was successfully extubated and moved to the ward. The family subsequently discovered the DNACPR form and asked that it be removed, which was done. Unfortunately, Mrs Tracey deteriorated further and, after discussions with the family (Mrs Tracey was clear at this point that she did not want to discuss resuscitation herself), a second DNACPR form was

completed: Mrs Tracey died on 7 March 2011 without attempted CPR.

The family subsequently instituted legal proceedings against the hospital, alleging that Mrs Tracey had two DNACPR orders imposed on her without being informed or consulted. The doctors at Addenbrooke's insisted that they had discussed this matter with both the patient and her family. However, because this discussion was not documented in the hospital notes, the High Court Judge Nicola Davies ruled that this conversation had not taken place. Judge Davies, however, declined to hear legal arguments about a breach of human rights, and the family took their case to the Court of Appeal in 2014. Lord Dyson, the Master of the Rolls, said this: 'since a DNACPR decision is one which will potentially deprive the patient of a life-saving treatment, there should be a presumption in favour of patient involvement. There need to be convincing reasons not to involve the patient.' Addressing the issue of doctors not involving patients in these decisions because it would cause distress, Dyson made sure that doctors are damned if they do, and damned if they don't: 'Whether it is appropriate to consult will depend on a difficult judgement to be made by the clinicians... There can be little doubt that it is inappropriate... to involve the patient in the process if the clinician considers that to do so is likely to cause her to suffer physical or psychological harm.' He threw in a lawyerly get-out clause, however: 'doctors should be wary of being too ready to exclude patients from the process on the grounds that their involvement is likely to distress them.'

What worries me about this case is the lack of understanding, on the part of both the Tracey family and the judiciary, of what cardio-pulmonary resuscitation is about. Any doctor would immediately conclude that resuscitation of a patient with Janet Tracey's combination of diseases and injuries was pointless, but Lord Dyson, and the Tracey family, clearly thought it was a potentially 'life-saving treatment'. Where the doctors and nurses at Addenbrooke's Hospital saw only futility and indignity, the Tracey family saw euthanasia. The final judgment was a sub-Beckettian farce: doctors were ruled to have breached the human rights of a patient by not having a conversation she explicitly did not want to have.

The Tracey judgment will have a profound effect on medical practice in Britain. Stories about DNACPR orders had been appearing regularly in the press even before the Tracey ruling. The usual theme of these stories was of families finding out that their elderly relatives had been subject to a DNACPR order without their knowledge, with the implication that this was a form of back-door euthanasia. These stories fed the same hysteria that led to the end of the Liverpool Care Pathway. I suspect the

Tracey family was familiar with these stories, but what such families fail to understand is that when a doctor raises the resuscitation issue, it is usually because that doctor believes that such treatment would be ineffective. (I have witnessed this at close range when my father died.) Not offering resuscitation doesn't mean giving up on *all* treatment: it simply means not offering one particular treatment which is not going to work. It is possible that communication between the Tracey family and the doctors was poor. 'Poor communication' is usually blamed for this kind of stand-off, but I wonder.

In the wake of the Tracey case, all of the professional bodies with a stake in resuscitation (the Resuscitation Council, the British Medical Association, the Royal College of Nursing) made pious obeisance to the importance of 'communication'. My own experience has taught me that all the communication in the world is sometimes to no avail. Many with power over public opinion (the media, the judiciary) operate far from the messy realities of hospital life, and don't have to live with the consequences of their actions. Lord Dyson's ruling seems to be based on an assumption that all patients and families are like him – educated, informed and reasonable. 'Informed consent', as I have written, is a legalistic fantasy, as well as a convenient trump-card in negligence proceedings. Luckily – and remarkably – most families are indeed reasonable, but a significant minority are not. And these families, inflamed by the newspapers and the abstract notion of their 'rights', will demand treatments, no matter how unreasonable or futile they are. Hospital doctors, already exhausted and demoralized, will acquiesce, and full resuscitation will be the default setting. The Tracey ruling, I predict, will result in many more dying people undergoing CPR as their final experience on this earth.

The Tracey family are quietly satisfied that 'some good' has come out of Janet's death. Her husband David said this after the Court of Appeal judgment: 'It feels as though the wrong done to Janet has been recognized by the court and the fact that her death has led to greater clarity in the law gives us all some small comfort.' Maurice Saatchi, too, fervently hoped that 'some good' would emerge from his bereavement. Saatchi's attempt to 'find some good' thankfully failed, but the Traceys' equally wrong-headed campaign was successful.

As for the judiciary, I am reminded of a lawyer friend who advised me: 'If you go to court, don't expect justice, or common sense, expect law.' Decisions that doctors used to routinely make themselves are now being made by the courts, and judges are likely to become increasingly involved in medical decisions relating to end-of-life care. An eighteen-year-old boy had been treated for many years at an English hospital for a brain tumour, but his doctors eventually concluded in 2015 that further treatment, in particular chemotherapy, would be pointless. His parents were unwilling to accept this, and went to the High Court in an attempt to overturn their decision. The Court, on this occasion, supported the doctors, and the boy died shortly after. But in another case, in June 2015, the Court of Protection in London ruled that St George's Hospital must continue to treat, fully and actively, a 'deeply religious' Muslim man left severely brain-damaged after a cardiac arrest. I could list many more: such cases now appear regularly in the newspapers. Are we facing a future where families who disagree with doctors will routinely go to court to get their own way? I must correct myself: that 'future' is already here. Julia Neuberger's warning about doctors and nurses becoming 'the whipping boys for our inadequate understanding of how we die' is not, as she imagined, a 'risk', something that might happen in the future: it is a neat summary of what is happening now.

Matt Cooper, the Irish journalist and broadcaster, wrote about how difficult it was – particularly as an only child – to discuss resuscitation with doctors when his parents were dying. If someone as articulate and knowledgeable as Cooper finds this hard, for many families it will be impossible, even intolerable. And I'm not sure that we, as doctors, should dump these decisions on relatives: in most cases, it is a discussion that doesn't need to happen. In England, however, the Tracey ruling has ensured that this discussion is now compulsory.

KILL ME

Philippe Ariès wrote in *The Hour of our Death* about the temptation of suicide, 'one of the last temptations in the *artes moriendi*: "Go ahead and kill yourself" suggests the devil to the sick man who is already lifting his dagger'. Ariès quoted the French social scientist Claudine Herzlich, who asked: 'Are people going to demand to die when *they* are ready to die?' Herzlich's dystopian future has arrived.

Marie Fleming, who died in December 2013, became famous in Ireland as a 'right to die' campaigner. She had, over many years, become progressively more incapacitated by multiple sclerosis (MS). She and her partner, Tom Curran, went to the High Court, and subsequently the Supreme Court, to establish her right to die, in particular for her partner to actively assist in killing her, without fear of prosecution. She lost her case, but became something of a national heroine. She died some months after the Supreme Court hearing. After her death, Tom Curran said: 'She died peacefully at home, in her own bed, and that is what she was fighting for.'

It is difficult to write objectively about Marie Fleming without appearing to be disrespectful of the dead, and those who grieve for them, but had Marie Fleming succeeded, she would have altered forever the way in which I practise my profession. For that reason alone,

I feel I have the right to comment on her case and its wider implications. But first this should be said: Marie Fleming did not need to 'fight' for the death which eventually took her. No law stopped her from dying 'peacefully at home, in her own bed'. In her memoir, *An Act of Love*, Tom Curran writes in the Foreword:

> Her fame spread around the world as she went to the highest court in Ireland in an attempt to establish her right to take control away from the MS in determining the time and manner in which she died. To her, this was the ultimate fight against the beast that had taken so much from her. She was determined that the MS would not control her death as it did much of her life – and her concern was not just for herself but for others in similar situations to us. And, while she had the assurance from me that she could be in control at the end, the court case was an attempt to protect those who were prepared to help her. While she may have lost the case, she ultimately won in the end.

One word dominates this paragraph: control. Marie Fleming's memoir begins: 'My last request on this earth is to be allowed to die at home in the arms of my partner, Tom, and with my two adult children, Corrinna and Simon, close by. I want to be held, hugged and whispered to as I pass on... I had to take the state to court.'

Fleming had several close encounters with death in the years running up to the court case. It appears that Nature offered Marie Fleming an exit on more than one occasion, but she declined this offer: 'When I had pneumonia and nearly died, Tom asked me if I wanted to be saved or not. I chose to be saved. The time was not right.' She wanted a death where she would expire in the arms of her partner, with her two children in attendance. This recalls Philippe Ariès's description of the 'Beautiful Death' of the Romantic era: 'an occasion for the most perfect union between the one leaving and those remaining behind'. Fleming and Curran initially had some naïve ideas about assisted suicide: 'When I first told him that I wanted him to help me, *he hoped we could call on a doctor to administer an injection* [my italics], but this was not to be. It was going to be a difficult process both from a physical and a legal point of view.'

The couple considered going to the Dignitas clinic in Switzerland, but decided against it. Instead, they resolved to take on the state. Fleming was eager for such a stage: 'I have never had a voice. As a child, when I was trying to be a mother to my siblings and my father, I tried shouting for help, but nobody heard me. When I was pregnant, I took an overdose but nobody listened. I hope the court will give me that voice I have always craved.'

On her first day at the High Court, one of her barristers posed the following question to her: 'And what about palliative care? Have you thought of going into a hospice to die?' Fleming replied: 'That is not acceptable to me.' The court was sympathetic; the president of the High Court of Ireland, Nicholas Kearns, remarked that Fleming was 'in many ways the most remarkable witness which any member of this court has been privileged to encounter'. The judgment, however, went against her: 'The court did not agree that my rights under the Constitution negated the ban on assisted suicide.' The wording of the Court's judgment read: 'While a competent adult patient has the right to refuse medical treatment, even if this leads to death, the taking of active steps by a third party to bring about the death of another is an entirely different matter...'

The couple appealed to the Supreme Court, but lost. The judgment, however, seemed to suggest that some special arrangement might be found for Marie Fleming:

> Justice Susan Denham did say, and I quote, that 'nothing in the court's judgment should be taken as necessarily implying it would not be open to the state, in the event the Oireachtas [the Irish Parliament] were satisfied that measures with appropriate safeguards could be introduced, to deal with a case such as that of Ms Fleming's.' I didn't find much comfort in that.

Following the Supreme Court judgment at the end of April 2013, Tom Curran made an emotionally charged appearance on *The Late Late Show*, Ireland's long-running television chat show. He read out a letter from Marie Fleming: 'Thank you for listening to what I have to say. This is what was missing from the court. While I feel let down by the judgment, it is more upsetting that it feels I wasn't listened to.'

Marie Fleming died at home in December 2013, seven months after the Supreme Court judgment. Tom Curran was the only one with her at the end: 'Marie died exactly the way she wanted to die – peacefully at home in my arms.' The Irish state paid most of the 'substantial' legal costs.

The Marie Fleming story is a curious one. At its heart, there is an obsession with control. Fleming, before the onset of MS, had a somewhat troubled life. Her mother abandoned the family when Marie was a child, and she had to become mother to her siblings. She became pregnant as a teenager. There was an overdose. Two marriages failed. She admitted that she hoped that her High Court appearance would give her 'the voice she always craved'. And it did: she became famous, an Irish heroine. The media coverage was almost unanimously supportive of her case and she was described as brave, courageous, clear-minded and an inspiration. But, as I suspect the various judges who ruled on her case surmised, the law is also there to protect the cowardly, the stupid, the unloved and the uninspiring.

Marie Fleming was fighting not for the right to die, but for the right to die on her own, highly individualistic, terms. She did not want an unpredictable death, its timing and manner decided by nature, but instead a death entirely scripted and controlled by herself. What's wrong with that? Nothing, if it concerns Marie Fleming only. But had she won her court case, the Irish Constitution would have had to be amended. Vulnerable, sick, old people, with little thought of a stage-managed demise, would have suddenly found themselves with a new 'option'. Doctors would suddenly have been faced with a new 'role'.

Her story is also instructive on another level. Media coverage, as I have said, was almost unanimously in her favour, and dissenting views were not heard. Suffering was conflated with moral infallibility; it became unacceptable to disagree with someone who was the victim of a progressive and incurable disease. Those who have suffered are regarded as having a special moral authority. We can acknowledge, and sympathize with, Marie Fleming's suffering, but we cannot, as a society, alter our laws to indulge the fanciful notions, held by a single individual, of a special death.

Tony Nicklinson, like Marie Fleming, also went to the High Court (the English one) for the right to assisted suicide. Like Fleming, he lost his case. He died in August 2012, days after the High Court rejected his plea for a doctor to help end his life. After the verdict, he refused food. 'The official cause was pneumonia,' said his widow Jane, 'but really it was a broken heart. He got the decision and deteriorated within a day or two. He just gave up.' Clearly, she saw no irony in the situation: he died of frustration because a court had denied him the right to die. In a further bizarre twist, Jane Nicklinson continued to wage a legal battle on behalf of her husband – a dead man – for the right to die. Her appeals were rejected by both the Supreme Court and the European Court of Human Rights. Nicklinson, just like Marie Fleming, wanted the right to die according to *his* script. It wasn't really about suffering, or death as such: it was again about control. Both Fleming and Nicklinson were left physically powerless by their diseases; was dictating the manner of death their only means of exerting any control?

Jeffrey Spector died at the Dignitas clinic in Switzerland in May 2015. He spent his last week being filmed by a television crew. He had been diagnosed with a spinal tumour six years before: the tumour was inoperable and would eventually have paralysed him. When he noticed some loss of sensation in his fingers, he decided, according to the *Guardian*, that 'he wanted to be in control of the final stages of his life'. His family begged him to reconsider, but for Spector, a successful businessman, control was what really mattered. His tumour was slowly progressive – he had lived with it for six years – and it is possible that he might have enjoyed several more years of independent life. What would Jeffrey Spector say to Richard Ford?

The campaign in support of assisted dying seems to be founded on a rather naïve view of human nature, and supported by the views and experience of exceptional individuals. I have encountered enough dodgy families and, indeed, dodgy doctors (such as the proto-Harold Shipman I met back in 1980), to feel nothing but relief at the Marie Fleming verdict.

Suicide pacts, where the two participants 'assist' each other, usually without outside intervention, are also instructive. Sometimes, as in the case of the philosopher Seneca and his wife Paulina, things do not go to plan: the suicide was botched – he died, but she did not. Another example, which has always disturbed me, is the case of the Hungarian émigré writer Arthur Koestler and his wife, Cynthia. Koestler had written about death frequently, and resolved to take his own life in his seventies when he became ill with Parkinson's disease and leukaemia. He wrote a suicide note, which ended – almost as an afterthought – with: 'My wife decided that after thirty-four years of working together, she could not face life after my death.' As far as we know, Cynthia was in good health and not suffering from any psychiatric disorder, when she and Koestler took a fatal combination of alcohol and barbiturates in 1983. It is not entirely surprising that Koestler, who had a particular view on the role of women (as well as a huge ego and a domineering, powerful personality), should write on behalf of his wife and allow her to end her life on the rather specious grounds that 'she could not face life' without him. After a suitable period of Geoffrey Gorer-type mourning, she might very well have changed her mind. She might have survived to reflect on her late husband's monstrous egotism. Cynthia Koestler, alas, was not as fortunate as Paulina. Koestler needed not only to control the manner of his own death, but also to drag his wife with him, in a grotesque secular take on the Hindu practice of suttee.

Cicely Saunders observed that those asking for assisted suicide fall into three camps: (1) 'Treat my pain'; (2) 'Let me die'; and (3) 'Kill me' (now/later – usually later). Groups 1 and 2 are asking for a solution to a problem that is soluble by means other than killing them. This leaves a minority in Group 3. Many people in this group – Jeffrey Spector would be a good example – are used to being in control over most aspects of their lives, so it is understandable that they wish to exert the same degree of control over their deaths.

Nearly all the cases invoked in support of assisted suicide are of eloquent, intelligent people. But, as we have seen, the majority of dying patients placed on the

Liverpool Care Pathway did not even know they were dying. 'The life of the poor man', observed Philippe Ariès, 'has always been an ineluctable fate over which he has no control.' But what might conceivably be right for Marie Fleming or Tony Nicklinson may not be good for society at large: normalizing killing coarsens society.

Baroness Mary Warnock is an eminent academic moral philosopher, and a fine exemplar of the British intellectual establishment. She holds refreshingly unfashionable views on people with dementia:

> If you're demented, you're wasting people's lives – your family's lives – and you're wasting the resources of the National Health Service… I'm absolutely fully in agreement with the argument that if pain is insufferable, then someone should be given help to die… I think that's the way the future will go. Putting it rather brutally, you'd be licensing people to put others down.

Her comments, unsurprisingly, caused outrage, but Warnock is old enough, and patrician enough, to not give a damn. Although I admire her insouciance and élan, she is, of course, deluded. Warnock has spent most of her life in Oxford Common Rooms, far from the realities of nursing homes and geriatric wards. I worked in the NHS for many years, and never once did I encounter a patient who raised a concern that they might be wasting its finite resources. Feeling one is a burden to the state is something that the ancient Spartans may have known, but not modern Britons. Mary Warnock also fails to understand that dementia is a spectrum of illnesses: at the bad end, there are people who are mute, incontinent, suffering; at the other end, are people with some degree of memory loss, who need a little help, but whose quality of life is good.

I am worried about a future when doctors are licensed 'to put others down'. I am worried about what some families would get up to if given formal powers as 'advocates'. I am worried about what some biddable and obliging doctors would get up to if given such licences. Between Mary Warnock on one side of the argument, and the over-enthusiastic, anti-ageist doctors on the other side, lies a middle path for people with dementia. You don't have to allow licensed doctor-executioners to euthanize them, but at the same time you don't have to treat all acute illnesses, such as pneumonia. We can provide comfort and care without killing people and without overburdening the health service. Assisted suicide is not a 'slippery slope': it's a paradigm shift.

The US state of Oregon enacted the Death with Dignity Act in 1997, which allows terminally ill people to obtain prescriptions for lethal doses of barbiturates, which they administer themselves. Nearly twenty years after the act became law, only three in every 1,000 people dying in Oregon avail themselves of this freedom. One third of those given a lethal prescription never use it. Twenty of 460 dying people regurgitated the drug, and one patient took a record 104 hours to die. 'The doctors we talked to said it was likely she just had a very strong heart', remarked George Eighmey, executive director of Compassion, a voluntary group which 'supports and monitors' Oregonians given these prescriptions. Another patient woke up after being asleep for 65 hours; according to Eighmey, he woke up 'because he had taken a laxative to mask the bitter taste of the legal drug, which prevented his body from absorbing the drug quickly enough.' He died, we are told, two weeks later, unassisted.

Some opponents of assisted suicide argue that vulnerable groups, such as the poor, the uneducated, and people with chronic physical or mental disability might be susceptible to this kind of death. A 2007 study examined the experience in Oregon and the Netherlands, and found no evidence for this claim. The only group with 'a heightened risk' was people with AIDS. I am not remotely surprised by the findings of this study. The passion for control is rare among the 'vulnerable'.

The doctor in me is vehemently opposed to assisted suicide, but another part of me is (slightly) attracted to the idea of having the freedom to end one's own life. Perhaps if I wasn't a doctor, I might even be a supporter of assisted suicide. I am wary, however, of the notion of 'death-on-demand' as a glib riposte to the inevitable miseries of old age. The modern gospel of the 'compression of morbidity' is partly to blame. This concept was popularized by Dr James F. Fries, Professor of Medicine at Stanford University Medical School, who first wrote about his theory in 1980. Put simply, the 'compression of morbidity' teaches that as longevity increases, old age will be a period – increasingly longer – of active life and good health, followed by a short, relatively painless, final illness. American baby-boomers, bombarded with images of jogging octogenarians, have invested heavily in this concept, and are desperate for it to be true. Unfortunately, it isn't. Study after study has shown that rising longevity is accompanied by increased disability, social isolation and loss of independence. Half of all Americans spend their last year in a nursing home. Is the demand for assisted suicide partly fuelled by disappointment that the 'compression of morbidity' is a fairy-tale, that old age is not always an unbroken run of golden years?

I have described the two extremes of control – 'kill me' and 'don't let me die' – but both are delusions. In the end, nature will decide.

CHAPTER 8

To Philosophize is to Learn How to Die

A long-held (and almost completely unchallenged) assertion of philosophy is that it prepares one to meet death with equanimity. Socrates and Seneca taught that we should not fear death, that we can overcome the dread of it by keeping it constantly in our thoughts. I have never been persuaded by this. The great popularizer of this idea was Montaigne. Michel de Montaigne (1533–92) was a French nobleman who, at the age of thirty-eight, withdrew from public life and spent the remaining twenty years of his life reading, thinking and writing what he called 'essays'. He is usually credited with inventing this literary form. His essays were like nothing that had ever been written before: highly personal, speculative, uninhibited, discursive and inspired by his reading of the great classical authors. His parents had engaged a Latin tutor for Montaigne, who spoke the language fluently before he could converse in his native French. He was thus deeply influenced by the writings and examples of Cicero, Seneca and Marcus Aurelius.

The young Montaigne had a busy career as a magistrate, civil servant and diplomat. He was obsessed by death: as a young man, he lost his friend and soulmate, Étienne de la Boétie (who died of plague), and six years later his younger brother Arnaud died after a freak accident (a brain haemorrhage caused by a blow to the head from a tennis ball). Of his six children, only one survived into adulthood. Montaigne resolved to adopt the Stoic approach to death; his famous essay 'To philosophize is to learn how to die' borrowed its title from Cicero, who in turn, borrowed it from Socrates. The Stoics taught that we should face the inevitable with courage, resignation and lack of fuss. Fate cannot be controlled, but one's attitude to events, including death, can: 'At every moment let us picture it in our imagination in all its aspects. At the stumbling of a horse, the fall of a tile, the slightest pin prick, let us promptly chew on this: Well, what if it were death itself?'

But Montaigne was forced to re-examine his beliefs after a dramatic incident which occurred when he was thirty-six. He was thrown from his horse, and sustained serious injuries. Lying in a semi-conscious state, Montaigne was surprised to find himself experiencing no fear or pain. He was convinced that he would die yet felt completely at peace: 'in truth not only free from distress but mingled with that sweet feeling that people have who let themselves slide into sleep'. Miraculously, Montaigne survived and had a slow and painful recovery. This event completely changed his attitude to death: 'If you don't know how to die, don't worry; Nature will tell you what to do on the spot, fully and adequately. She will do this job perfectly for you; don't bother your head about it.' Sarah Bakewell, in her biography of Montaigne, *How to Live* (2010) wrote: '"Don't worry about death" became his most fundamental, most liberating answer to the question of how to live. It made it possible to do just that: *live*.'

DO PHILOSOPHERS DIE BETTER?

Do philosophers, and those authors (such as Tolstoy) who write about death, die any better than their less contemplative brethren? My rather banal conclusion is this: some philosophers die well, some die badly; they appear to have no particular advantage over non-philosophers.

Montaigne maintained, purely on the basis of his own near-death experience, that dying is easy, and convinced himself for the remainder of his life that death was not to be feared. This was a neat psychological trick, but if accounts of his demise are accurate, it was not at all easy, although he did it bravely. He died of quinsy, or peritonsillar abscess, at the age of fifty-nine. He had previously expressed the wish that he would die while 'planting cabbages'. It was not to be. He died slowly and painfully, over several days, propped up in bed. He struggled for breath, and his entire body was grotesquely swollen. In one of his essays, Montaigne had written that the most horrible death would be to have one's tongue cut out, to be without the power of speech. His illness did just that.

His was the typical public death described by Philippe Ariès: Montaigne's family, servants and priest were in attendance. Having written his will, Montaigne, although not an especially devout man, had a last mass said in his room. He died during this mass, probably of suffocation, as the abscess slowly closed off his windpipe. This was precisely the kind of death he had hoped to avoid:

> ...the cries of mothers, wives, and children; the visits of astounded and afflicted friends; the attendance of pale and blubbering servants; a dark room, set round with burning tapers; our beds environed with physicians and divines; in sum, nothing but

ghostliness and horror round about us; we seem
dead and buried already...

The painter Joseph-Nicolas Robert-Fleury depicted
Montaigne's death in *Les derniers moments de Montaigne*
(1853). The canvas shows those very 'terrible ceremonies
and preparations', right down to the dark room and the
pale and blubbering servants. Montaigne has left us
many well-polished phrases about not fearing death, but
his philosophizing did not prevent him from having the
type of death he expressly wished to avoid.

Montaigne tells us little of practical value about
dying, because dying in sixteenth-century France was so
different to what we experience now. Dying in old age
was unusual in Montaigne's day, but now it is the norm.

Some philosophers, such as Hume and Wittgenstein,
do indeed die a 'philosopher's death'. Others, like Albert
Camus (1913-60), died in character: he was killed in a
car crash, having ditched plans to make the journey by
train. The unused train ticket was found in his coat-
pocket. He had once remarked that he couldn't imagine
a more meaningless death than dying in a car accident.
'So Camus died in a car with a train ticket in his pocket,'
wrote Michael Foley in *The Age of Absurdity*, 'an absurdist
parable on the consequences of accepting someone
else's route.'

David Hume (1711–76), the great Scottish Enlightenment philosopher and historian, was, by universal consent, the most even-tempered and agreeable of men. Jules Evans, in *Philosophy for Life* (2012), recounts the story of his death:

> In his sixties, after a long and distinguished career as an essayist, historian and philosopher, Hume fell ill with a disorder of the bowels that was probably cancer. His friend, the philosopher Adam Smith, tells us that Hume initially fought the disease. But the symptoms returned, and 'from that moment he gave up all thoughts of recovery, but submitted with the utmost cheerfulness, and the most perfect complacency and resignation' to his death.

Hume's final illness lasted long enough – sixteen months – for him to write a brief autobiography, *My Own Life*:

> I have suffered very little pain from my disorder; and what is more strange, have, notwithstanding the great decline of my person, never suffered a moment's abatement of my spirits; insomuch, that were I to name the period of my life, which I should most choose to pass over again, I might be tempted to point to this later period.

Hume was an atheist and believed that death meant

extinction. He was not, however, an evangelical unbeliever in the Richard Dawkins mode; indeed, like Gibbon, he thought that one should maintain the religious proprieties, particularly when dealing with women and servants. Thomas Boswell visited him near the end, and was perplexed by Hume's equanimity: 'I asked him if the thought of annihilation never gave him any uneasiness. He said not the least, no more than the thought that he had not been, as Lucretius observes.'

The bioethicist Franklin G. Miller contrasted Hume's death with that of Christopher Hitchens. They were of a similar age when they died (Hume was sixty-five and Hitchens sixty-two) and had a similar interval between the onset of sickness and death (sixteen months and nineteen months respectively). Both believed that death meant oblivion. Because medicine in Hume's day had so little to offer, he spent this sixteen months writing his autobiography, and 'was exposed to none of the rigors and distressing side-effects of disease-fighting interventions'. Hitchens's nineteen months, as we have seen, were spent in 'Tumortown'. 'It is much more difficult today', concluded Miller, 'to achieve the tranquillity of Hume in facing death from cancer.'

Hume's calm deportment in the face of death is matched only by Ludwig Wittgenstein (1889-1951). In *The Book of Dead Philosophers* (2008), Simon Critchley tells the story of his final months:

After he had been diagnosed with terminal cancer, news that he apparently greeted with much relief, Wittgenstein moved in with Dr and Mrs Bevan... In the remaining two months of his life, he wrote the entire second half of the manuscript that was published as *On Certainty*... He had developed a friendship with Mrs Bevan; they would go to the pub together every evening at six o'clock where she would drink port and Wittgenstein would empty his glass into the aspidistra plant. She presented him with an electric blanket on his birthday and said, 'Many happy returns.' Wittgenstein replied, staring back at her, 'There will be no returns.' Mrs Bevan stayed with Wittgenstein during the last night and when she told him that his friends would be visiting the next day, he said to her, 'Tell them I've had a wonderful life.'

Ernest Becker was visited in hospital before his death by the philosopher Sam Keen:

The first words Ernest Becker said to me when I walked into his hospital room were: 'You are catching me in extremis. This is a test of everything I've written about death. And I've got a chance to show how one dies, the attitude one takes. Whether one does it in a dignified, manly way; what kind of thoughts one surrounds it with; how one accepts his death...'

Montaigne's hero, Seneca (4 BC–AD 65), was that rare entity, a vastly wealthy Stoic philosopher. He fell foul of his former pupil, the emperor Nero, and was ordered to take his own life. He and his wife Paulina resolved to die together and used the traditional Roman method of cutting their veins and soaking in a bath. This didn't work, because the veins stopped bleeding. Seneca eventually died from suffocation in a steam bath. The whole episode was grisly, messy and protracted; hardly the dignified exit of a Stoic. The game and willing Paulina survived – Nero had sent orders forbidding her death, so her wounds were bandaged. She went on to live for many more years. Is there a lesson here? Perhaps if Arthur Koestler's wife Cynthia had read about Paulina, she might not have been so enthusiastic about the death-pact with her husband. Even Seneca, with all his wisdom, experience and wealth, couldn't carry off the classical Stoic death. His botched demise was marked more by farce than nobility.

Johann Wolfgang von Goethe (1749–1832), widely acclaimed as the wisest man of his age, lived to eighty-two, productive almost to the end. His friend, the poet Johann Peter Eckermann, wrote in *Conversations of Goethe*: 'The morning after Goethe's death, a deep desire seized me to look once again upon his earthly garment.

His faithful servant, Frederick, opened for me the chamber in which he was laid out. Stretched upon his back, he reposed as if asleep; profound peace and security reigned in the features of his sublimely noble countenance.' His doctor's diary, however, revealed that Goethe, at the end, was 'in the grip of a terrible fear and agitation'. Goethe's last words were famously: '*mehr Licht*' ('more light'). The Austrian novelist Thomas Bernhard wrote a short story, 'Claim', about a man who claimed at every opportunity that Goethe's last words, were, in fact, '*mehr nicht*' ('no more'). For his persistence, this man was eventually incarcerated in a lunatic asylum. Goethe's close friend, Friedrich Schiller (1759–1805), fell ill with pneumonia and died. Goethe had been sick at the same time, but recovered. Schiller's last words, in the throes of pre-terminal delirium were: '*Ist das euer Himmel, ist das euer Hölle?*' ('Is that your heaven, is that your hell?') Goethe and Schiller were buried alongside each other in Weimar.

Philip Larkin dismissed the claims of both religion and philosophy:

> This is a special way of being afraid
> No trick dispels. Religion used to try,
> That vast moth-eaten musical brocade
> Created to pretend we never die,
> And specious stuff that says *No rational being*
> *Can fear a thing it will not feel...*

Larkin died in hospital in Hull. Like Christopher Hitchens, he had oesophageal cancer and was in his early sixties (sixty-three). A friend visiting him the day before he died said: 'If Philip hadn't been drugged, he would have been raving. He was that frightened.'

The novelist Elizabeth Jane Howard once told Julian Barnes that the three most death-haunted people she had known were Larkin, Kingsley Amis and John Betjeman. In his poem 'Late-Flowering Lust', the cuddly Poet Laureate chillingly confessed that a love affair in middle age merely served to remind him of the inevitable:

> I cling to you inflamed with fear
>> As now you cling to me,
> I feel how frail you are my dear
>> And wonder what will be –
>
> A week? or twenty years remain?
>> And then – what kind of death?
> A losing fight with frightful pain
>> Or a gasping fight for breath?

But the death-haunted Betjeman, in the end, was luckier than he had anticipated. He died peacefully in Treen, the house in Trebetherick, Cornwall, which he had loved so much. Betjeman's long-time lover, Elizabeth Cavendish, wrote to a friend:

...he died on the most beautiful sunny morning with the sun streaming into the room & the French windows open & the lovely smell of the garden everywhere & Carole [Betjeman's nurse] was holding one of his hands & me the other & he had old Archy [his teddy-bear] & Jumbo in each arm & Stanley the cat asleep on his tummy.

A. N. Wilson, in his biography of Betjeman, observed: 'There was a perfection in his dying where he had spent so many childhood hours of happiness.'

Somerset Maugham (1874–1965) learned much about death and suffering during his five years as a medical student at St Thomas's Hospital in London. On the hospital wards and in the slums of Lambeth (where he worked as an obstetric clerk), he witnessed many deaths, and found nothing noble about it:

> I set down in my note-books, not once or twice, but in a dozen places, the facts that I had seen. I knew that suffering did not ennoble; it degraded. It made men selfish, mean, petty and suspicious. It absorbed them in small things. It did not make them more than men; it made them less than men; and I wrote ferociously that we learn resignation not by our own suffering, but by the suffering of others.

Although he never practised as a doctor, Maugham's experience as a medical student formed his world-view, which was that people weren't much good, and life was meaningless. Maugham's own end was messy, protracted and undignified. He lived to ninety-one, but his final years were scarred by dementia and violent mood swings. Interviewed by the *Daily Express* on the occasion of his ninetieth birthday, he said he longed for death: 'I am drunk with the thought of it. It seems to me to offer the final and absolute freedom.' The story is told (it may be apocryphal) that Maugham, nearing the end, summoned the philosopher A. J. Ayer to his home on the Riviera, the Villa Mauresque. He asked Ayer, a resolute atheist, to reassure him that there was no afterlife. Ayer was happy to oblige. More than twenty years later, Ayer had a near-death experience after choking on a piece of salmon. He admitted that this experience provided 'rather strong evidence that death does not put an end to consciousness'. Ayer's wife, Dee, told Jonathan Miller: 'Freddie has got so much nicer since he died.'

Tolstoy (1828–1910) showed unique psychological and spiritual understanding of dying in his fiction, but his own death was undignified and unedifying. At the age of eighty-two, he finally summoned the courage to leave his wife, Sonia. Their relationship had been deteriorating for several years, not helped latterly by the constant presence at his country estate, Yasnaya Polyana, of Tolstoy's 'disciples'. The great novelist crept out in the dead of night, but quickly fell ill with pneumonia, and died a few days later in the station-master's house in the railway station of the rural town of Astapovo. A swarm of journalists and cameramen descended on the little town in a media scrum; at least six doctors kept separate records of his final illness, and Tsarist spies reported back to St Petersburg.

George Orwell (1903–50) described the horrors of hospital death in his essay 'How the Poor Die' (1946), after a spell as a patient in the Hôpital Cochin in Paris in 1929. He died in 1950 in University College Hospital in London, having suffered from pulmonary tuberculosis for many years. In his biography of Orwell, Bernard Crick wrote that he was not aware that he was dying. At the time of his death, he was making plans to travel to a Swiss sanatorium and his main concern was the quality of the tea he might be offered there: 'They have that filthy Chinese stuff, you know. I like Ceylon tea, very strong.' Orwell died at night, alone, following a lung haemorrhage.

Sigmund Freud died in London in 1939, having fled Vienna the year before. Over a period of sixteen years, he had undergone over thirty operations and several courses of radiation. He was seeing patients up to two months before his death. Towards the end, Freud's dog, a chow called Lün, could not bear to be in the same room as his master because of the stink from Freud's necrotic tumour. His physician, Max Schur, had followed Freud to London, and kept his promise: 'When he was again in agony, I gave him a hypodermic of two centigrams of morphine. The expression of pain and suffering was gone. I repeated the dose after about 12 hours. Freud was obviously so close to the end of his reserves that he lapsed into a coma and did not wake up again.' At the end, Schur, as he had promised, was Freud's *amicus mortis*.

The combination of virtues shown by Hume and Wittgenstein – courage, nobility, intellect and an unflinching acceptance of the truth – are rare indeed. Seneca, Goethe, Maugham and Tolstoy, for all their insight into death and dying, died themselves no better than the unlettered vulgarians. There have doubtless been many anonymous and uncelebrated folk throughout history (such as Montaigne's peasant neighbours) who died as bravely and as nobly as Hume and Wittgenstein. Being a philosopher or a thanatologist clearly confers no special advantage. Sarah Bakewell concluded of Montaigne: 'Philosophers find it hard to leave the world because they try to maintain control. So much for "To philosophise is to learn how to die." Philosophy looked more like a way of teaching people to *un*learn the natural skill that every peasant had as a birthright.'

So, is philosophy a waste of time, impotent to temper the terror of death? Some writers less exalted than Montaigne and Seneca may have more relevant things to say to us about death. Montaigne did not conduct interviews with the dying, but Bronnie Ware, an Australian palliative care worker, did, and wrote a bestselling book called *The Top Five Regrets of the Dying: A Life Transformed by the Dearly Departing* (2012). These top five are: (1) I wish I'd had the courage to live a life true to myself, not the life others expected of me; (2) I wish I hadn't worked so hard; (3) I wish I'd had the courage to express my feelings; (4) I wish I'd stayed in touch with my friends; (5) I wish I'd let myself be happier. Ware argues that our denial of death causes us to lead inauthentic lives: 'we carry on trying to validate ourselves through our material life and associated fearful behaviour instead. If we are able to face our own inevitable death with honest acceptance, before we have reached that time, then we shift our priorities well before it is too late.'

The French psychologist Marie de Hennezel also worked for many years in palliative care, and also wrote a best-seller, called *Seize the Day* (2012), with the same message: 'Death can be a door that opens to a greater awareness and a more meaningful life.' The trick, of course, is to come to this conclusion when you are still healthy.

Julian Barnes wrote about the 'lemon table' at the Kämp restaurant in Helsinki, where, in the 1920s, local intellectuals, including the composer Sibelius, would gather to discuss death. The lemon was the ancient

Chinese symbol of death, and those seated at this particular table were obliged to discuss this – and no other – topic.

I have my own version of the lemon table. The largest cemetery in Cork, St Finbarr's, is a short walk from the hospital where I work. I regularly visit St Finbarr's, usually at lunchtime, particularly when the weather is good. I started visiting the cemetery not because of any Montaignian intention to contemplate death, but because it is a restful, quiet place, ideal for a short walk in the middle of the working day. St Finbarr's is so large that I walk only a small section at a time. There is a long, wide, tree-lined avenue, flanked by two Romanesque chapels, with several smaller, numbered, paths leading off it. The Republican plot is situated just inside the main entrance gate, and contains the graves of the local heroes, such as Tomás MacCurtain and Terence MacSwiney, who died in the War of Independence. The cemetery was built in the mid-nineteenth century and initially accommodated mainly the professional and merchant classes. Many headstones proudly list the degrees and professional qualifications of the deceased. Nearly all famous Corkonians are buried in St Finbarr's; the only notable exceptions being Michael Collins (buried in Glasnevin in Dublin) and the blues guitarist Rory Gallagher, whose plot is in the new cemetery, St Oliver's, where my father is also buried.

My interest, however, is in the unknown, the unheroic and the neglected. Each row of headstones tells a few brief stories of heartbreak: here, the young surgeon, dead at thirty – what happened? There, the child dead at fifteen, his father joining him less than two years later. Next, the girl I knew at school, who died of leukaemia aged just seventeen. (Her mother had been to see me as a patient, and I told her that I had known his long-dead daughter. Her eyes filled with tears as I told her.) Most of the plots are tidy and well maintained; a few are neglected and overgrown, the lettering on the headstones now indecipherable. One well-kept plot commemorates a woman who died aged forty-three in 1884, 'To the inexpressible grief of her husband and children'. Wittgenstein would have understood. The plot containing the remains of the local Franciscan monks has a headstone on which is engraved a phrase of St Francis's: 'Welcome, Sister Death'.

When I last visited St Finbarr's, on a fine, windy autumn day, I heard my name called from the other side of the cemetery wall. It was K., a classmate from primary school. He was standing on a ladder, thinning a tree in a garden adjoining the cemetery. K. had started working as a landscape gardener when he was made redundant, after twenty-eight years, from his job at a local factory. I retrieved for him some of the branches that had fallen on the plots below; we talked amiably about getting older, children leaving home, and how it all went by so fast. A visit to St Finbarr's is a reliable antidote to work-related worry; half an hour spent in the company of the dead is surprisingly soothing.

THE CONSOLATIONS OF FAITH

Philippe Ariès observed how, in medieval Europe, death was seen as a transition to another life. Religion, not medicine, was the guiding force: nobody expected medicine, as we do now, to cure them when they fell mortally ill. Much of our contemporary fear of death is attributable to the prevailing certainty, for most people, that death means extinction, oblivion. One would think, intuitively, that death and dying would be less terrifying for those with a strong religious faith. But I do not believe that this is so. The US, ostensibly the most God-fearing nation on earth, is also the most death-fearing. A palliative care colleague told me how commonly priests experience profound spiritual crises when they are dying. The story is told of a cardinal who, when diagnosed with terminal cancer, confided in a saintly fellow priest. The priest congratulated the cardinal and expressed some envy that he would soon be with God and his angels. This priest is presented to us as a sort of holy fool, but isn't this exactly how a true believer should react to such news?

J. G. Ballard wrote of Francis Bacon's series of 'pope' paintings (inspired by Velásquez's portrait of Pope Innocent X): 'His popes screamed because they knew there was no God.'

Unlike Bacon's popes, my uncle – the priest – truly believed. Did his faith sustain him when he was dying? I think so. Although he was ninety and had endured a miserable year or more, he was frightened of dying. He did not fear death but, rather, dying alone. Although his supple mind was well acquainted with theology and philosophy, he had the simple, unshakeable faith of country people. He firmly believed that physical death was the portal that opened into eternal life. When it became clear that he was dying, family members took it in turns to sit with him. For the last twenty-four hours, he was semi-conscious, anaesthetized by the syringe-driver. In his final agony, he called out: 'I want to go home.' Home, for him, was always Dromore, the place he had left more than seventy years before. Dromore had always held for him a mystical, almost religious, fascination. Honour thy father and thy mother: he revered his parents and prayed daily that he would rejoin them in Heaven.

The eldest of his three surviving sisters, a nun, sat with him, hour after hour, and prayed. Exhausted, she was eventually persuaded by my brother to take a break and have a meal. My wife (Scottish Catholic) and sister-in-law (Bavarian Lutheran) took her place, and he died shortly after. My aunt bitterly regretted missing the moment of his death. Shortly after, the family gathered around him in the room and said the Rosary. His funeral was a lavish, public affair, which would not have shamed a head of state.

My father-in-law, too, was sustained by his faith. A few days before he died, the parish priest came to give him the Last Rites, and hear his confession. He told the priest that he didn't want to die, but was ready.

My own generation, let down both by organized religion and frenetic materialism, does not enjoy the consolations of faith. The Ireland I grew up in was a theocracy in all but name; the Ireland I came back to in 2001 reminded me of 'Pleasure Island' in Disney's *Pinocchio*. In the space of a generation, the power of the Catholic Church had collapsed, probably forever. Shortly after that, the chimera that was the Celtic Tiger disappeared. The resulting spiritual and moral vacuum has not been filled. Fear of death has replaced fear of God.

HOW DOCTORS DIE

Medical knowledge is, or should be, a huge advantage when facing death. We know how it goes. We can decode the smooth words of the oncologist. We understand the implications of any given diagnosis. This should help – shouldn't it? Did Kieran Sweeney's knowledge make it any easier for him? I like to think that when faced with my own inevitable endgame, my medical knowledge will at least spare me the indignities of self-delusion and futile treatments. I wonder. A 2003 study from Johns Hopkins University examined doctors' preferences for their own care at the end of life. Most had an advance directive. The overwhelming majority did not want cardio-pulmonary resuscitation, dialysis, major surgery or PEG feeding. They were unanimous in their enthusiasm for analgesic drugs. The uncomfortable conclusion of this study is that doctors routinely subject their patients to treatments that they wouldn't dream of having themselves. The Kansas-based pathologist Dr Ed Friedlander proudly sports a tattoo on his chest saying 'No CPR'.

An American doctor, Ken Murray, wrote an article called 'How Doctors Die' in 2011:

> Years ago, Charlie, a highly respected orthopedist and a mentor of mine, found a lump in his stomach. He had a surgeon explore the area, and the diagnosis was pancreatic cancer. The surgeon was one of the best in the country. He had even invented a new procedure for this exact cancer that could triple a patient's five-year survival odds – from 5 per cent to 15 per cent – albeit with a poor quality of life. Charlie was uninterested. He went home the next day, closed his practice, and never set foot in a hospital again.

He focused on spending time with family and feeling as good as possible. Several months later, he died at home. He got no chemotherapy, radiation, or surgical treatment. Medicare didn't spend much on him.

It's not a frequent topic of discussion, but doctors die, too. And they don't die like the rest of us. What's unusual about them is not how much treatment they get compared to most Americans, but how little. For all the time they spend fending off the deaths of others, they tend to be fairly serene when faced with death themselves. They know exactly what is going to happen, they know the choices, and they generally have access to any sort of medical care they could want. But they go gently.

Not all doctors, however, display Charlie's matter-of-fact stoicism. A doctor acquaintance of mine, diagnosed with inoperable cancer, underwent several courses of chemotherapy, all of them complicated by horrific side effects, and believed right to the end that he would recover and return to his practice. He died on an acute medical ward, having refused to engage with the palliative care services, which he regarded as 'throwing in the towel'.

One of my former bosses, a distinguished academic, became suddenly very sick at the age of fifty-seven. He died in hospital within a few weeks, of unsuspected pancreatic cancer. After his death, the task of clearing out his office fell to one of his colleagues. He was notoriously disorganized and untidy, but, to his colleague's surprise, everything in the office was neatly filed. Clearly he had either known, or had a premonition of, his condition, but had told no one. The succession was easy and orderly.

Albert Camus thought that life was meaningless, its only consistent attribute being absurdity. Human beings torture themselves by trying to find meaning where there is none. Religion is the greatest expression of this quest for meaning. We look for meaning in everything: as children we look for patterns in clouds and paving stones. Life looks easier if it is viewed as a story with a narrative and a theme. Far from being terrified by this meaninglessness, Camus suggests that we should embrace it, because ultimately that is where freedom lies. Few of us, however, have the existential clarity and courage of Camus: having to be the author of your own script for living and dying is an intolerable burden for most modern secular people. We have fetishized choice but, like children, we long for boundaries and rules.

Death, as I have seen it, is more often marked by pain, fear, boredom and absurdity than it is by dignity, spirituality and meaning. What are we to do? Our problem with death is that, compared to our ancestors, we live so long. We know, in theory, that we must die, but we have banished death from our thoughts.

CHAPTER 9

Live For Ever

Rolf Zinkernagel, a Swiss immunologist who won the Nobel Prize in Physiology or Medicine in 1996, believes that the lifespan of human beings has far exceeded what it was intended for: 'I would argue that we are basically built to reach 25 years of age. All the rest is luxury.' Wealthy older Americans spend a lot of time and money maintaining their health and postponing death. Dinner-party conversations centre on colonoscopies, statins (drugs which reduce blood cholesterol) and new diets. Many lay Americans subscribe to the *New England Journal of Medicine*. I have noticed a similar trend in well-off, older acquaintances of mine: health, and its maintenance, has become their hobby. All quite laudable, but let's take this trend to its logical conclusion. What are the consequences for society if average life expectancy rises to a hundred, or even more? We have already seen radical changes to pension provision as life expectancy increases and the birth-rate (among white Europeans) falls. We face the prospect of an army of centenarians cared for by poorly paid immigrants. The children of these centenarians can expect to work well into their seventies, or even eighties. The world of work will alter drastically, with diminishing opportunities for the young.

What if powerful new therapies emerge which can slow down the ageing process and postpone death? Undoubtedly it will be the rich and powerful who will avail themselves of them. Poor people in Africa, Asia and South America will continue to struggle for simple necessities, such as food, clean water and basic health care. There will be bitter debates about whether the state should fund such therapies. The old are a powerful lobby group and, compared to the young, are far more likely to vote, and thus hurt politicians at the ballot box. We have seen politicians in the UK and Ireland performing U-turns on social provision for the old after concerted political action by that constituency. Politicians and policy-makers mess with welfare provision for the old at their peril. The baby-boomers of rich Western countries are now in their sixties and seventies, and are aiming for a different kind of old age to their parents. They demand a retirement that is well funded, active and packed with experience. They are unfettered by mortgage debt and are the last generation to receive defined benefit pensions. The economic downturn of the last several years has only strengthened their position. They are passionate believers in the compression of morbidity.

But this vision of ageing is wishful thinking. Many now face an old age where the final years are spent in nursing homes. There are several societal reasons for this: increased longevity, the demise of the multi-generational extended family and the contemporary obsession with safety. None of us wants to spend the end of our life in a nursing home; they are viewed (correctly) as places which value safety and protocol over independence and living. There have been several nursing-home scandals in Ireland over the last few years, which has led to demand for even tighter regulation and surveillance of these institutions. The use of hidden cameras (to monitor the staff) is now routinely proposed, on the grounds that inspections by government agencies are toothless, as the nursing homes are pre-warned of the inspectors' visit. The people who work in nursing homes – commonly poorly paid, uneducated immigrants – will find themselves under constant scrutiny. The surgeon and memoirist Henry Marsh observed how working in a long-stay dementia ward when he was a student taught him 'the limits of human kindness'. In Ireland, the nursing-home scandals have demonstrated these limits, yet we are outraged when the poor and uneducated strangers to whom we have subcontracted the task of caring for our old people are found wanting.

What are we to do? We will not see a return of the pre-industrial extended family; the future is urban, atomized and medicalized. The American bioethicist Ezekiel Emanuel (older brother of Rahm, Mayor of Chicago) outraged the baby-boomers with his 2014 essay for *The Atlantic*, 'Why I hope to die at 75'. He attacked what he called 'the American Immortal': 'I think this manic desperation to endlessly extend life is misguided and potentially destructive. For many reasons, 75 is a pretty good age to aim to stop. Americans may live longer than their parents, but they are likely to be more incapacitated. Does that sound very desirable? Not to me.'

Auberon Waugh (who died aged sixty-one), son of Evelyn Waugh (who died aged sixty-two), once remarked: 'It is the duty of all good parents to die young.' Montaigne put it like this: 'Make room for others, as others have made room for you.'

Charles C. Mann wrote an essay in 2005 for *The Atlantic* called 'The Coming Death Shortage', which envisaged a future 'tripartite society' of 'the very old and very rich on top, beta-testing each new treatment on themselves; a mass of ordinary old, forced by insurance into supremely healthy habits, kept alive by medical entitlement; and the diminishingly influential young.' Mann cites the case of Japan, where one in three men over the age of sixty-five is still in full-time employment; the Japanese are 'tacitly aware' that the old are 'blocking the door'. Meanwhile, one in three young adults is either unemployed or working part-time, leading lives of 'socially mandated fecklessness'. The American philosopher and physician Leon R. Kass predicts a future of 'protracted youthfulness, hedonism, and sexual licence'.

I am broadly in agreement with Kass and Mann that ever-increasing longevity is bad for society, but the problem is this: given the opportunity of a few extra years, would I take them? Of course I would. There is an old joke: 'Who wants to live to be a hundred? A guy who's ninety-nine.' And this problem of the interests of the individual clashing with the interests of society runs right through modern medicine, as we have seen with cancer treatment and assisted suicide. The menu of options is increasing all the time, and it looks so attractive.

We are familiar with the contemporary hubristic and bellicose use of military metaphor: the war on this, the battle against that. We regularly hear outlandish calls to arms: Prime Minister David Cameron has pledged that 'a cure for dementia' will be found within ten years. This is as likely to be successful as Richard Nixon's 'War on Cancer'. William Haseltine, Chief Executive Officer of

Human Genome Sciences, claimed in 1999 that 'death is nothing more than a series of preventable diseases'. However, neither the Human Genome Project nor stem-cell technology has so far delivered the cures that had been predicted, though biomedical research grows in size and scope. The biomedical research industry is just that: a business, not an exercise in altruism.

Medicine has taken much of the credit, but longevity in developed countries has increased owing to a combination of factors, which include not only organized health care, but also improved living conditions, disease prevention and behavioural changes, such as reductions in smoking. Interestingly, the maximum human lifespan has remained unchanged at about 110–120; it is average longevity which has increased so dramatically. Where do we draw the line and call 'enough'? We can't. John Gray has eloquently argued that although scientific knowledge has increased exponentially since the Enlightenment, human irrationality remains stubbornly static. Science is driven by reason and logic, yet our use of it is frequently irrational. Does this phenomenon have any relevance to my daily work as a doctor? Well yes, it does. Irrationality pervades all aspects of medicine, from deluded, Internet-addled patients and relatives, to the overuse of scans and other diagnostic procedures, to the widespread use of drugs of dubious benefit and high cost. Cancer care, as we have seen, has been described as 'a culture of medical excess'. Overuse and futile use is driven by patients, doctors, hospitals and pharmaceutical companies. The doctor who practises sparingly and judiciously has little to gain either professionally or financially.

RAISING THE DEAD

Technology ever increasingly fuels our utopian hunger. Sam Parnia, an English intensive care specialist working in New York, has written a book called *The Lazarus Effect* (2013). Parnia is an evangelist for a technique called Extracorporeal Membrane Oxygenation (ECMO), which is used to resuscitate people who have had a cardiac arrest. The blood of the patient is removed entirely, put through a membrane which oxygenates the blood, and pumped back into the body. The idea is to buy time while the problem that caused the arrest can be fixed. Parnia claims:

> It is my belief that anyone who dies of a cause that is reversible should not really die anymore. That is: every heart attack victim should no longer die. I have to be careful when I state that because people will say, 'My husband has died recently and you are saying that need not have happened'. But the fact is heart attacks themselves are quite easily managed. If you can manage the process of death properly, then

you go in, take out a clot, put a stent in, the heart will function in most cases. And the same with infections, pneumonia or whatever. People who don't respond to antibiotics in time, we could keep them there for a while longer [after they had died] until they respond.

Parnia's idea is very attractive in the case of say, a fifty-year-old man with cardiac arrest caused by myocardial infarction (James Gandolfini), or a footballer collapsing during a match with a disorder of the heart rhythm (Fabrice Muamba). However, were ECMO to become standard treatment and widely available, I could easily envisage frail, elderly, wealthy patients, dying of pneumonia (in theory, reversible), receiving this therapy. And this is the problem with every new exciting treatment: you can't be seen to ration it. Isn't the life of the old lady with pneumonia just as worth saving as that of Fabrice Muamba? And all death is ultimately preceded by the heart stopping: 'the one thing that is certain about all our lives', says Parnia, 'is that we will all eventually experience a cardiac arrest. All our hearts will stop beating.' The definition of illness that is 'reversible' is so vague that most dying patients could qualify for ECMO. This technology is highly likely to take root and flourish in America. The cost, financial and spiritual, is likely to be steep. And this technology blurs even further the line between life and death, a line that is becoming increasingly more difficult to identify.

Sam Parnia and William Haseltine's belief that death is mainly preventable, finds an echo in the contemporary reluctance on the part of doctors to write 'old age' as the cause of death in a death certificate.

John Gray, in his book *The Immortalization Commission* (2011), wrote about a prevailing belief in Victorian Britain and later, in Soviet Russia, that science could deliver immortality. He describes the bizarre attempts by the Soviet scientist Krasin to preserve Lenin's body, an undertaking that failed disastrously:

> [In] 1924, he constructed a refrigeration system designed to keep the embalmed cadaver cool. But the cryogenic technology failed to work, and the body began showing signs of decay... Told of these problems, Krasin was adamant the freezing could succeed. Any condensation that might be damaging the cadaver could be dealt with by installing double glazing and obtaining a better refrigerator from Germany, always the best source of technology in Bolshevik eyes. The German refrigerator was imported, but the process of deterioration continued...

Gray referred to cryonic suspension as a variety of 'techno-immortalism'. Ray Kurzweil, the American 'visionary' is a modern Krasin, and is currently engineering director of Google. In *Transcend: Nine Steps to Living Well Forever* (2009), he and his co-author, medical doctor Terry Grossman, suggest that a rigid regimen of diet, vitamin supplementation, regular exercise and preventive medicine could keep us going long enough until the time when technology can help us transcend our biological limitations, and give us a form of virtual immortality: 'if you stay on the cutting edge of our rapidly expanding knowledge, you can indeed *live long enough to live forever.*'

In *The Singularity is Near: When Humans Transcend Biology* (2005), Kurzweil claims that we are on the verge of a scientific revolution, which will allow us to 'remodel' ourselves. Tiny robots – 'nanobots', operating at a molecular level – will 'have myriad roles within the human body, including reversing human ageing (to the extent that this task will not already have been completed through biotechnology, such as genetic engineering)'. Fusing human and artificial intelligence will create an immortal entity, in which 'the non-biological portion of our intelligence will ultimately predominate'. Kurzweil currently leads a project called 'Calico', under the aegis of Google, a programme of medical and genetic research with the goal of 'ending ageing'. He has specified a time when this sudden acceleration in human knowledge could make immortality technically possible: 'I set the date for the Singularity – representing a profound and disruptive transformation in human capability – as 2045.' (I would then be eighty-five; if I keep myself alive until then, maybe I, too, could become an 'Immortal'.)

Kurzweil is not alone: there are many 'immortalists' and 'transhumanists' who believe that the technology which may dramatically lengthen human longevity is just around the corner. Perhaps the most famous of these is Aubrey de Grey, a Cambridge-based, self-taught biologist of ageing. Grey, who started as a computer scientist, is a proselytizer for what he calls 'Strategies for Engineered Negligible Senescence', a range of putative molecular therapies to prevent ageing.

It is entirely possible that de Grey and his fellow immortalists are right; but I disagree with their assumption that this is a good thing. Bryan Appleyard, in his book *How to Live Forever or Die Trying* (2007), has speculated on how a dramatic rise in longevity would affect our work, our relationships, politics, our sense of self, art, philosophy and religion. For meliorists – those who believe in the inexorable progress of mankind – prolongation of life and avoidance of death are core beliefs. The still-wealthy baby-boomers are enthusiastic believers; those who are sceptical have been dismissed as 'mortalists'. The boomers, the richest generation in human history, are most definitely not content to make room for the next generation.

Madeline Gins was an American artist and poet who died, aged seventy-two, in January 2014. She and her husband, the Japanese conceptual artist Shusaku Arakawa, were 'transhumanists' and believed that people died because they lived in surroundings that were too comfortable. They designed buildings which were uncomfortable enough to 'counteract the usual human destiny of having to die'. They called this philosophy 'Reversible Destiny'. Her obituary in the *Daily Telegraph* reported:

> Their ideas remained largely theoretical until 2005 when they unveiled a small apartment complex in the Tokyo suburb of Mitaka, known as the Reversible Destiny Lofts. Painted in lurid blues, pinks, reds and yellows, each apartment features a dining room with a warped floor, making it impossible to install furniture, a sunken kitchen and a study with a concave floor.

Gins and Arakawa invested all their money with Bernie Madoff, and Arakawa died in 2008. This sad little tale reminds me of the photograph of a dejected-looking man, posing with a huge, defrosted refrigerator, containing the mortal remains of his wife; he had hoped, at some unspecified future date, to have her resurrected by whatever technology would become available. An unanticipated electrical failure had dashed any such hope.

But not all transhumanists are deluded eccentrics.

There is a critical mass of sober, objective scientists who predict that the technology which could significantly extend our longevity is highly likely to become available in the coming decades. Advances in stem-cell biology and regenerative medicine may make organ replacement as routine as replacing a used battery. It is more likely, however, that maximum human lifespan will remain static at 110–120, and average life expectancy will increase dramatically, but only among the well-off and well-educated. Professionals retiring at sixty-five are now expecting thirty years of healthy, active retirement. The poor, even in developed countries, may experience a fall in longevity, mainly because of obesity and smoking. Meanwhile, the rich and well-informed, with the help of diet and exercise, screening for disease, and preventive medications, will fuss and jog their way to a hundred years old. For £125, the US company 23andMe will analyse your DNA for your risk for a variety of diseases. The CEO, Anne Wojcicki, is the estranged wife of Google co-founder, Sergey Brin. Brin's DNA tests showed a risk of Parkinson's disease. He responded to this news by 'increasing his coffee intake and intensifying his workout regimen', two factors thought to have a preventive effect against the disease.

St Paul believed that death was caused, not by inevitable biological decay, but by sin: 'Sin entered the world through one man, and through sin death, and thus death has spread through the whole human race because everyone has sinned.' St Anselm, writing in the eleventh century, also attributed death to human sinfulness:

> Moreover, it is easily proved that man was so made as not to be necessarily subject to death; for, as we have already said, it is inconsistent with God's wisdom and justice to compel man to suffer death without fault, when he made him holy to enjoy eternal blessedness. It therefore follows that *had man never sinned he never would have died* [my italics].

In our own post-Christian society, we have come to believe in a similar doctrine. But the sins are not those I learned about in my catechism as a child; the sins that cause death are not old-fashioned ones, such as avarice, sloth, gluttony, anger, lust and so on, but newer ones, such as smoking (now also an official Catholic sin), low fibre intake, lack of regular exercise, failure to take advantage of preventive measures against ill-health and 'internalizing' anger. Healthiness has become the new godliness.

TOO MUCH MEDICINE?

Many within medicine view with alarm the direction modern health care has taken. Much of what Ivan

Illich predicted in the 1970s (and which was dismissed at the time) has come to pass. Many health economists believe that spending on medicine in countries like the US has passed the tipping point where it causes more harm than good. We have seen the rise in the concept of disease 'awareness', promoted, not infrequently, by pharmaceutical companies. Genetics has the potential to turn us all into patients, by identifying our predisposition to various diseases. Guidelines from the European Society of Cardiology on treatment of blood pressure and high cholesterol levels identified 76 per cent of the entire adult population of Norway as being 'at increased risk'. This ruse of 'disease mongering' (driven mainly by the pharmaceutical industry) has identified the worried well, rather than the sick, as their market.

A growing resistance movement has taken root, with various strands to it, such as the Slow Medicine movement, founded in Italy in 1989, inspired by the Slow Food movement. At a meeting of the movement in Bologna in 2013, Gianfranco Domenighetti listed the characteristics of health systems as follows: 'complexity, uncertainty, opacity, poor measurement, variability in decision-making, asymmetry of information, conflict of interest, and corruption'. The British Medical Association has backed a 'Too Much Medicine' campaign, which shares some of the aims of the Slow Medicine movement. The 'Choosing Wisely' campaign in the US has created an evidence-based list of medical interventions that are frequently futile and unnecessary.

The founders of the NHS naïvely believed that a free health-care system would result in a healthier society, and thus less demand for its services. Enoch Powell, who held office as a health minister, was among the first to point out the fallacy of this argument. Ivan Illich coined the term 'Sisyphus syndrome', meaning the more health care given to a population, the greater its demand for care: 'I invite all to shift their gaze, their thoughts, from worrying about health care to cultivating the art of living. And, today, with equal importance, to the art of suffering, the art of dying.'

We cannot, like misers, hoard health; living uses it up. Nor should we lose it like spendthrifts. Health, like money, is not an end in itself; like money, it is a prerequisite for a decent, fulfilling life. The obsessive pursuit of health is a form of consumerism and impoverishes us not just spiritually, but also financially. Rising spending on health care inevitably means that we spend less on other societal needs, such as education, housing and transport. Medicine should give up the quest to conquer nature, and retreat to a core function of providing comfort and succour.

Julian Barnes's 1989 novel, *A History of the World in 10½ Chapters*, concludes with a parable about immortality. The narrator wakes: 'I dreamt that I woke up.' He is attended by a woman, 'like a stewardess on some airline you've never heard of', who brings him the most delicious breakfast he's ever eaten. It gradually transpires that he is in some form of paradisical afterlife, which will last for eternity. Every fantasy he has ever had comes true, and he indulges every desire he has ever had. He meets all the famous people he has ever admired, and even gets to have sex with them. (Barnes's paradise echoes the afterlife promised to Islamist suicide-bombers.) He completes every round of golf with eighteen shots. Eventually, he runs out of new experiences. He discovers, to his dismay, that most of his fellow occupants of this paradise ('Heaveners') tend to choose a second death – oblivion. 'It seems to me', the narrator remarks, 'that Heaven's a very good idea, it's a perfect idea you could say, but not for us. Not given the way we are.'

CHAPTER 10

Creatureliness

In our health, we have grand notions about how we shall face death, but it's rarely as we imagine, or plan. Daniel Callahan listed the components of a peaceful death: 'a death marked by self-possession, by a sense that one is ending one's days awake, *alert* [my italics], and physically independent... a time when friends and family draw near, when leave can be taken...' Christopher Hitchens, too, anticipated being conscious: 'Before I was diagnosed with esophageal cancer a year and a half ago, I rather jauntily told the readers of my memoirs that when faced with extinction I wanted to be fully conscious and awake, in order to "do" death in the active and not the passive sense.' Having witnessed the deaths of patients 'fully conscious and awake' (such as the man at Bradford Royal Infirmary, described in Chapter 1), I would not wish such an end on my worst enemy. When the end came, however, Hitchens had the modern cancer death, comatose for the last day or so. There were no Jamesian profundities or Voltairean bons mots.

'The painful riddle of death', wrote Freud, 'against which no medicine has yet been found, nor probably will be... With these forces nature rises up against us, majestic, cruel and inexorable; she brings to our mind once more our weakness and helplessness.' Perhaps the only sensible way of dealing with death is to accept this weakness and helplessness: what the philosopher Simon Critchley calls our 'creatureliness'.

TO DIE LIKE A DOG

One autumn evening, some years ago, I found a dying fox in my garage. He barely acknowledged my presence, and made no attempt at fight or flight. I left a bowl of milk for him. When I returned the next morning, he was dead. I buried him in the garden. To 'die like a dog' is shorthand for a kind of death which is stripped of 'dignity', 'spirituality' and 'meaning', but animals – if left alone – die better than humans. They find a quiet corner, turn their face to the wall, and wait.

Somerset Maugham, during his years as a medical student, saw many people die: 'And never have I seen in their last moments anything to suggest that their spirit was everlasting. They die as a dog dies.' To 'die like a dog'? I should be so lucky. I have observed that, compared to humans, the medical treatment of sick animals is characterized by common sense, humanity and realism.

Just a few months before he was diagnosed with cancer, Christopher Hitchens wrote an alternative Ten Commandments. His sixth commandment was: 'Be aware that you are an animal and dependent on the web of nature, and think and act accordingly.' I found this very poignant, not only because it is so true, but also because Hitchens forgot it when he became ill himself.

As a young man, Montaigne believed that the key to dealing with death was to study the Stoic philosophers of antiquity, and be guided by their teachings and example. He saw, however, that the local peasants, who were illiterate and knew no philosophy, died just as well as Socrates, and better than Seneca. Nature took care of them: 'I never saw one of my peasant neighbours cogitating over the countenance and assurance with which he would pass his last hour.' Tolstoy also observed that unlettered Russian peasant folk, the *narod*, accepted death as the will of God:

These people accept sickness and grief without

question or resistance but calmly, in full certainty that this had to happen and could not be otherwise, it was all for the good... these people live, suffer and approach death with a tranquil spirit, more often than not with joy... a difficult, complaining and unhappy death is the ultimate rarity among the common people.

WHAT'S A LITTLE TROUBLE?

'I don't want to be a burden' is a sentiment often expressed by people with worries about dying, but seldom, I have observed, by the dying themselves. Yet being a burden is what our creatureliness is all about, it's what makes us human. Being a burden is the antithesis of contemporary atomization and aggressive individualism. We should want to be a burden to those who love us, and they should want to bear that burden.

In Tolstoy's *The Death of Ivan Ilyich*, the dying man becomes isolated from his immediate family, who maintain the pretence, almost to the end, that he will recover, that he is not dying. This loneliness compounds his suffering. Only Gerasim, Ilyich's peasant servant, is willing to attend to his master's bodily functions and suffering. He is not offended by the notion of cleaning his master; he understands creatureliness:

Gerasim alone did not lie; everything showed clearly that he alone understood what it meant, and saw no necessity to disguise it, and simply felt sorry for his sick, wasting master. He even said this once straight out, when Ivan Ilyich was sending him away.

'We shall all die. So what's a little trouble?' he said, meaning by this to express that he did not complain of the trouble just because he was taking this trouble for a dying man, and he hoped that for him too someone would be willing to take the same trouble when his time came.

Philippe Ariès observed how increasing squeamishness around bodily functions was one of the factors that caused death to become 'hidden': 'It is no longer acceptable for strangers to come into a room that smells of urine, sweat and gangrene, and where the sheets are soiled. Access to this room must be forbidden, except to a few intimates capable of overcoming their disgust, or those indispensable persons who provide certain services.'

When Susan Sontag was dying, the only person she could speak candidly to was a lowly nursing assistant – like Gerasim, one of 'those indispensable persons who provide certain services'. The dying man needs to be cared for like a little child, and, like a little child, sometimes needs to be relieved of responsibility. Tolstoy described how Ivan Ilyich, too, wanted to be treated like a child: 'At certain moments, after prolonged suffering, Ivan, ashamed as he would have been to own it, longed more than anything for someone to feel sorry for him, as for a sick child. He longed to be petted, kissed, and wept over, as children are petted and comforted.'

TURNING TO THE WALL

To 'turn to the wall' is an ancient, biblical, gesture of the dying. The dying withdraw from the living: 'In those days was Hezekiah sick unto death. And Isaiah the prophet the son of Amoz came to him, and said unto him, Thus saith Jehovah, Set thy house in order; for thou shalt die, and not live. Then Hezekiah turned his face to the wall, and prayed unto Jehovah' (Isaiah 38).

To 'turn to the wall' when dying was thought to be a sign of secret adherence to Jewish religious practices amongst the Marranos, the Jews of Spain and Portugal who were forcibly converted to Christianity during the Middle Ages. The dying, to this day, still turn to the wall. My father-in-law, in his final weeks, withdrew. His immediate family was hoping for some form of engagement, 'closure' or acknowledgement from him that he was dying, but his instinct was to slowly shut down.

Over twenty years ago, a close family friend became suddenly ill. She was admitted to hospital and was found to have multiple cancer deposits ('metastases') throughout her liver. She was a heavy smoker, so this cancer had probably originated in her lungs. She had lost her husband to cancer twenty years before; she knew how things went with this. A liver biopsy was performed, and the diagnosis was confirmed. The oncologist suggested chemotherapy; she declined. This gregarious woman turned her face to the wall, refused to see visitors and was dead within a few days.

The writer and critic Cyril Connolly, twenty-five years before his death, prescribed 'a cure for the fear of death, to be taken *logically*' for a woman friend who had expressed this fear. He, like Hume, quoted Lucretius to the effect that 'Death therefore does not exist, neither does it concern us a scrap.' Twenty-five years later, his friend Anthony Hobson noted in his diary: 'He [Connolly] is dying without fuss or emotion, like an ancient Roman, philosophically, stoically.' Connolly's biographer, Jeremy Lewis, describes his last day: '...when Stephen Spender came to see him, very near the end, he turned his face to the wall and whispered "Who is it? Is it Stephen? Go away – I no longer belong to this world."'

We turn to the wall, as animals do, as our ancestors did.

'DEATH WITH DIGNITY'

Philippe Ariès was contemptuous of the modern approach to dying, which he thought too neat, too glib, an unwillingness to recognize and acknowledge the awesome power of death: 'they propose to reconcile death with happiness', he observed acidly. Modern Western culture seeks to package death, to manage and process it, to re-tame it, but in a modern way. 'Death with dignity' and a 'good death' have become the contemporary slogans and perceived entitlements, but what exactly do they mean? We all anticipate, and long for, 'death with dignity', a 'spiritual' death, but most people do not experience that. Dying not only dismantles our body, but also our personality and spirit. We expect too much of the dying. They are too tired, too spent, to be 'spiritual', to do 'death with dignity'. The noble death, the spiritual death, is the exception. For this to happen, you need a unique personality and special circumstances. I am not at all sure what 'death with dignity' means. In the US, it has become a euphemism for euthanasia. In Britain, the phrase is routinely trotted out when assisted dying is debated. The hospice movement – so territorial over death – holds up 'death with dignity' or the 'good death' as its aim, but I don't believe that we can prescribe a 'good death'.

What elements are required for a dignified death?

The phrase 'death with dignity' implies a recognition that dying has begun and the withdrawal of 'active' medical treatment. Dying in an ICU is for most people the antithesis of 'death with dignity', but, as we have seen, dying in an ICU is not as undignified as we imagine. Terror is undignified, but terror can be conjured away by the syringe-driver, so Ivan Ilyich's three days of relentless screaming is now a rare experience.

A prerequisite of a dignified death is recognition and an acceptance, by the dying man, his family and his doctor, that death is taking place. This is not as easily dealt with as terror or pain, and many die without this recognition and acceptance. A logical progression from recognition and acceptance is the notion of leave-taking: the formal acknowledgement by the dying man that he must leave his family and this life, a handing over to those left behind. The leave-taking was a key component of the 'tame death' of the distant past, but is now vanishingly rare. The syringe-driver has rather done for last words. Nowadays we hope for a different kind of going: to die in our sleep. In the era of tame death, such a death – one without warning – was accursed: the *mors repentina et improvisa*.

There are more humble components of dignity, such as attention to, and tact around, bodily functions; an ambience in the ward of quiet and decorum – as I have shown, in general hospital wards this can be extraordinarily difficult to achieve. Modern medicine makes 'death with dignity' difficult and, for many, unattainable. The frail old woman sent in from the nursing home with pneumonia does not die with dignity in the resuscitation room of the Emergency Department. Dementia does not afford many opportunities at the end, for dignity – nor does technological brinkmanship. But above all else, 'death with dignity' is difficult because modern medicine does not regard care of the dying as a core aspect of its mission. Because so many of us die of chronic disease, it can be difficult to be certain when dying has begun. And any disease, at any stage, is potentially treatable: something – anything – can always be done, no matter how futile.

The notion of 'death with dignity' may be more for the benefit of families than for the dying themselves. It is not acceptable for family and carers to express irrita- tion and impatience with the dying, but these emotions are commonly experienced. Caring for a dying person at home, perhaps for many months, is exhausting and tedious. For both the dying and their families, moments of tenderness (or even 'spirituality') are far fewer than the periods of despair, loneliness and terror. The dying may unsportingly fail to behave with dignity and courage; they may become, as Maugham observed, 'selfish, mean, petty and suspicious'. 'Death with dignity' may simply reflect an aspiration on the part of those witnessing death, for less mess, less odour. Death – or at least the process of dying – offends, as Tolstoy observed, our notions of propriety. In hospital, the dying fail to fit in with our timetables. Relatives, with their many professional and family commitments, are disappointed to learn that the doctor cannot predict the time of death with any great accuracy. The dying wax and wane in their dying: bad on Monday, a little better on Tuesday. Their courage waxes and wanes too: one day accepting and peaceful, the next consumed with terror and denial. Insight and acceptance, too, fluctuates. On Monday, the dying man may acknowledge that death is imminent, and that further treatment is futile. On Tuesday, however, he may become suddenly enthused about a novel anti-cancer drug, or a clinic in America with amazing results. The dying just don't follow the script laid out for a 'death with dignity'. But eventually, inevitably, nature, or the syringe-driver, takes control. If it is nature, the dying turn their faces to the wall, like any other animal. If it is the syringe-driver, they float away in a drug-induced oblivion.

Family members, too, may find their courage fails them when death is close. The more guilty the family member, the more likely they are to report a 'spiritual' experience: 'he appeared to be asleep, but when I came in, he raised his hand, almost as if he was giving me his blessing'. Unlike my aunt, some relatives do not want to be with the dying man at the moment of death, and may resort to all sorts of delaying tactics, such as getting 'stuck in traffic', to miss that moment.

We can only expect dignity in dying if we have shown dignity in living. The idea of 'death with dignity' is also informed by the modern view of each human life as a story – a 'narrative'. This concept has a powerful hold on the modern imagination, but may be a delusion. We are not one, but many selves. Which self should be mourned? It must be a terrible burden on the dying person to 'die in character', and by extrapolation, with 'dignity'. What if your dying day happens to be an 'off' day? What if you just don't have the physical or psychic energy to follow the narrative laid out for you? In novels, death is portrayed as the logical, inevitable conclusion to the life that has led up to it. Of course, life (and death) just isn't like that. There is no core personality; it alters over time and within time. This explains why the cowardly sometimes die well and the brave sometimes die badly. Those who are most attached to their own personalities find it hardest to die.

Death may not be the inevitable conclusion to the broad narrative sweep of one's life. It is more commonly banal – just another episode. Perhaps the idea of 'death with dignity' is yet another manifestation of our unwillingness to accept meaninglessness, both of life and of death. More importantly, we, as a species, have come to believe that everything that happens to us – including death – is our fault, our doing, our responsibility. Human agency has replaced the powers of nature, 'majestic, cruel and inexorable.'

FIRE FROM HEAVEN

Alexander the Great, of all figures from history, embodies the aristocratic ideals of nobility, courage, dignity and style. His death is perhaps the greatest example from history of dying as one has lived. In 323 BC, at the age of thirty-two, Alexander fell mortally ill in Babylon. There has been much debate as to the nature of this illness: theories include malaria, schistosomiasis, endocarditis, influenza, strychnine poisoning, alcoholic liver disease, and acute pancreatitis. Although I am not an adherent of the 'who-killed-Cock-Robin?' school of medical history, it was probably typhoid fever. Over a period of ten days, his condition steadily deteriorated. On the day of his death, his soldiers mobbed the gates of the palace, and suspecting that his death was being concealed from them, demanded to see him for themselves. Alexander instructed that the entire army be admitted, in single file, to his chamber. It was his final order and last parade. Although he was mortally weak, and probably in great pain, he greeted each one of them – they must have numbered in the tens of thousands – with a nod of his head, or a flicker of his eyes. The parade lasted for several hours.

Mary Renault, author of the *Alexander Trilogy* (*Fire from Heaven, The Persian Boy, Funeral Games*) – surely the greatest sequence of historical novels ever written – wrote a short biography, *The Nature of Alexander*, based on the classical histories of Plutarch, Curtius and Arrian. She describes how Alexander died as he had lived:

> Ever ready to die in war, he must long have been pre-pared to die in pain, and resolved it should not diminish him. The exhaustion must have shortened his last hours, but it is unlikely that at this stage he could have recovered. The necessary suffering he accepted in return for what had been essential to him all his life: to be equal to his legend; to be beloved; and to requite it extravagantly, regardless of expense. Whether sustained by pride, by philosophy, by belief in the immortality of his fame or of his soul, he met his end with no less dignity, fortitude and consideration for others than Socrates himself...

Sisygambis, mother of the defeated Persian Great King, Darius, was nominally Alexander's prisoner. She and Alexander formed a close friendship: he admired her nobility and courage, and addressed her as 'Mother'. She saw in her Macedonian conqueror all the kingly qualities her own son lacked. Mary Renault concludes her biography thus: 'Sisygambis, the Queen Mother of Persia, survived the news of his [Alexander's] death five days. On receiving it she bade her family and friends farewell, turned her face to the wall and died by fasting.'

Alexander's equanimity in his final days may have been, in part, a result of his belief that he was divine. After his death, he did achieve a kind of divinity, when he was worshipped as a god. But this sort of death is remarkable in its rarity, as were the less exalted, but no less noble, deaths of Hume and Wittgenstein. Most of us do not possess the spiritual or intellectual stature of these men. We need to have less lofty ambitions for death: such as a death without terror, a death without futile medical intervention, a death that is not hidden from the dying, a dying that takes place with a degree of respect and decorum.

Even so, death cannot be sanitized, work-shopped or managed. In death, there is only affliction. When our time comes, let us say our goodbyes and die as creatures. If we choose to turn to the wall, to withdraw from our families and the world, then there is no shame in that. The dying have turned to the wall since the time of Isaiah. And we who attend the dying must accompany them. We must not avert our gaze. Doctors must once again return to their role as the *amicus mortis*. And let us not hesitate to be brave.

Some Modest Proposals

Death has been a regular presence in my life, professionally and personally, over the past few years. What have I learned? I have concluded that I am – in the phrase of F. E. Smith – no wiser, but considerably better informed.

The contemporary discussion on death and dying has been hijacked by the extremists on both sides. In the barren and neglected middle ground are truths that we have conveniently ignored. As contemporary issues, assisted suicide and advance directives are both a symptom of a deeper malaise (namely, the obsession with control) and a distraction. They are a distraction because the real issues are elsewhere. Our sense of common decency – of kindness – has become sclerosed. Can common decency be regenerated by regulation and government diktat? We have witnessed, to our cost, the paradoxical effects of the regulation of professionals, as well as the poisonous effects of targets.

Modern scientific medicine, for all its achievements, has never been so unsure of itself. After the glory era of the mid-twentieth century, we are now in a late period of doubt and uncertainty: medicine has lost its nerve. It is in desperate need of reform – spiritual renewal might be a better term. And the reforms I mean are not the anodyne statements about professionalism piously promoted by the various august medical bodies. Medicine has slowly, almost imperceptibly, been transformed from a profession into a service industry. After thirty-two years of practice, I find myself out of step with many of my colleagues. I have witnessed a profound disconnect between our publicly-proclaimed pieties and what we actually do every day in our treatment of the dying, which is notable not for kindness, but for cowardice, evasion and humbug.

I have described the culture of medical excess, and the resistance movement against it. This movement, however, is patchy, under-subscribed and disorganized. There is a danger, too, that when you question the prevailing medical culture, you can find yourself unwittingly in the same tent as the Gerson Therapy faddists and the anti-vaccine campaigners. We must, as a profession, call a halt to the madness that characterizes much of modern medicine. The leaders in cancer medicine set a good example with the publication of The Lancet Oncology Commission Report in 2011. We must teach the public, the politicians, the media and the judiciary that we can't offer every conceivable option to every patient. The era of scientific triumphalism is over. Medicine needs to embrace a new phase, characterized by thoughtfulness and a creaturely approach to our patients.

But kindness should be a common currency for all – not something to be doled out solely by the professionals. Could the perceived 'problem' with death be partly due to the fact that, after decades of our culture being dominated by individualism and consumerism, our respect for other people has diminished? We have witnessed the paradox of rising life expectancy accompanied by a contemporary culture obsessed with youth and beauty, and dismissive of the old. The arid spiritual dwarfishness of materialism and secularism has hardly helped. We see ourselves, in the phrase of Ivan Illich, as 'bundles of diagnoses'. In Europe, the churches have emptied, and people no longer know how to die, or how to mourn. In my own country, this process has happened so quickly that we are still reeling.

There is a perception – even a consensus – that death is something that medicine should somehow 'sort out'. But our needs are spiritual, not medical. Medicine's dominion should be limited and explicitly defined. Medicine, and our culture, would be healthier and happier if we stopped expecting medicine to solve our existential and spiritual problems, if we stopped thinking of our bodies as machines, and if we gave up our fantasies of control and of immortality. Doctors can indeed help the dying, but dying needs to be de-medicalized. I was, in part, prompted to write this book because my limited, strictly medical, expertise was inadequate to meet the demands placed on it by society and by my dying patients and their families. I had no answers, no profound insight. It is as difficult to advise someone how to die, as it is to advise them how to live.

Acknowledgements

Maurice Earls read an early draft and persuaded Jonathan Williams to act as my agent. Jonathan's wisdom and experience were invaluable. My editor Neil Belton championed the book, and gave wise counsel over several revisions. Georgina Blackwell guided me through the publishing process with much common sense and patience. The manuscript was copyedited with great care and attention to detail by Jane Robertson.

Several friends and colleagues helped me to clarify my ideas: I would like to thank particularly Tony O'Brien, Eoin O'Brien and Columba Quigley. I am grateful also to Fr Michael Buckley, Dan Collins, Sheila Lordan, Anne Nagle and Brian O'Brien. My wife Karen provided unstinting moral support, as well as much practical assistance.

I have changed some of the details relating to patients to preserve confidentiality.

Glossary

amicus mortis	(Latin) death friend
ars moriendi	(Latin) the art of dying
bronchoscopy	endoscopic examination of the lungs
Cheyne-Stokes respiration	a pattern of breathing commonly observed in the dying
chondrosarcoma	malignant bone tumour, arising from cartilage
cirrhosis	permanent scarring of the liver, commonly caused by alcohol
Clostridium difficile	a bowel infection, usually caused by antibiotics
concierge doctor	a private physician with a small clientele, permanently on call for his or her patients
CPR	cardio-pulmonary resuscitation
cystic fibrosis	inherited lung condition; commonly causes premature death
DNACPR	Do Not Attempt Cardio-pulmonary Resuscitation
endoscopy	internal examination of bodily organs (stomach, bowel, lungs) using a flexible tube (endoscope)
High Dependency Unit (HDU)	a hospital ward for patients requiring close monitoring.

	HDU patients are not as unstable as those requiring intensive care.
Hospital Standardized Mortality Ratio (HSMR)	a statistical tool to calculate the number of 'expected' deaths in a hospital
intubate	to place a tube in the patient's airway, to facilitate artificial ventilation
kinesiology	a form of alternative medicine based on testing muscle strength
Liverpool Care Pathway	a care pathway which guided treatment of dying patients in English hospitals
locked-in syndrome	a type of stroke affecting the brain stem. The patient is aware, but almost completely paralysed
metastasis	secondary cancer deposit in another body organ
motor neurone disease	a chronic neuro-degenerative disease, which causes progressive weakness and wasting of muscles
myelodysplastic syndrome	a form of bone marrow cancer
myocardial infarction	coronary artery thrombosis (clot) leading to death of heart muscle
PEG tube	Percutaneous Endoscopic Gastrostomy. A feeding tube placed directly into the stomach cavity through the abdominal wall
propofol	commonly used anaesthetic drug
syringe-driver	a small infusion pump used to deliver a continuous supply of painkilling and sedative drugs
thanatology	the study of death

Bibliography

Adams, Tim (2013) 'Sam Parnia – the man who could bring you back from the dead.' *Observer*, 6 April.

Appleyard, Bryan (2007) *How to Live Forever or Die Trying*. London: Simon & Schuster.

Ariès, Philippe (1981) *The Hour of our Death*, translated by Helen Weaver. New York: Alfred A. Knopf.

Armstrong, Karen (2009) *The Case for God: What Religion Really Means*. London: The Bodley Head.

Asher, Richard (1972) *Talking Sense*. London: Pitman Medical.

Bakewell, Sarah (2010) *How to Live: A Life of Montaigne in One Question and Twenty Attempts at an Answer*. London: Chatto & Windus.

Ballard, J. G. (2008) *Miracles of Life*. London: Fourth Estate.

Ballard, Mark (2013) 'Data fear caused Mid-Staffs panic.' Online at http://www.computerweekly.com/blogs/public-sector/2013/03/data-fear-caused-mid-staffs-pa.html

Ballatt, J. and P. Campling (2011) *Intelligent kindness. Reforming the culture of healthcare.* London: RCPsych Publications.

Barnes, Julian (1989) *A History of the World in 10½ Chapters.* London: Jonathan Cape.

——(2008) *Nothing to be Frightened of.* London: Jonathan Cape.

Battin, Margaret P., Agnes van der Heide, Linda Ganzini, Gerrit van der Wal, Bregje D. Onwuteaka-Philipsen (2007). 'Legal physician-assisted dying in Oregon and the Netherlands: evidence concerning the impact on patients in "vulnerable" groups'. *Journal of Medical Ethics* 33:591–597.

Bauby, Jean-Dominique (1997) *The Diving Bell and the Butterfly,* translated by Jeremy Leggatt. London: Fourth Estate.

Becker, Ernest (1973) *The Denial of Death.* London: Souvenir Press (2011 edition, Foreword by Sam Keen). First published New York: Basic Books.

Beckford, Martin (2008) 'Baroness Warnock: Dementia sufferers may have a "duty to die".' *Daily Telegraph,* 18 September.

Bernhard, Thomas (1998) *The Voice Imitator,* translated by Kenneth J. Northcott. Chicago: Chicago University Press.

Betjeman, John (1958). *Collected Poems.* London: John Murray.

Bradley, Nick (2010) Obituary: Kieran Sweeney. *British Medical Journal* 340:c733 (8 February).

Bunker, J. P. (1997) 'Ivan Illich and the pursuit of health.' *Journal of Health Service Research and Policy* 2:56–59.

——(2003) 'Ivan Illich and medical nemesis.' *Journal of Epidemiology & Community Health*, 57:927.

Callahan, Daniel (2000) *The Troubled Dream of Life: In Search of a Peaceful Death.* Washington, DC: Georgetown University Press.

Campbell, Denis (2013) 'Mid Staffs hospital scandal: the essential guide.' *Guardian*, 6 February.

Camus, Albert (1975) *The Myth of Sisyphus*, translated by Justin O'Brien. London: Penguin Books. (First published as *Le Mythe de Sisyphe*, 1942.)

Carrier, Dan (2015) 'Man who killed himself at Dignitas explains decision in film.' *Guardian*, 26 May.

Charon, Rita (2001) 'Narrative Medicine: A Model for Empathy, Reflection, Profession and Trust.' *Journal of the American Medical Association*, 286(15): 1897–1902.

Chochinov, Harvey Max, Thomas Hassard, Susan McClement, Thomas Hack, Linda J. Kristjanson, Mike Harlos, Shane Sinclair, Alison Murray (2008) 'The Patient Dignity Inventory: A Novel Way of Measuring Dignity-Related Distress in Palliative Care.' *Journal of Pain and Symptom Management*, 36(6):559–71.

Clearkin, R.J. (2010) Good death for all remains distant goal. *British Medical Journal* 341:c5815.

Cohen, Lewis (2014) 'How Sigmund Freud Wanted to Die.' *The Atlantic*, 23 September.

Cooper, Matt (2015) 'I was twice asked the most difficult question an only child can face.' *Irish Daily Mail*, 14 January.

Crick, Bernard (1980) *George Orwell: A Life*. London: Secker & Warburg.

Critchley, Simon (2008) *The Book of Dead Philosophers*. London: Granta Books.

de Botton, Alain (2012) *Religion for Atheists*. London: Penguin Books.

de Hennezel, Marie (2012) *Seize the Day: How the Dying Teach us to Live*. London: Macmillan.

Department of Health (2010) *Robert Francis Inquiry into Mid-Staffordshire NHS Foundation Trust*. London: Department of Health. Online at www.dh.gov.uk/en/ Publicationsandstatistics/Publications/Publications

——(2013) *More Care, Less Pathway. A Review of the Liverpool Care Pathway*. London: Department of Health. Online at www.Gov.uk/government/publications/review-of-the-liverpool-care-pathway-for-dying-patients.

Diem, Susan J., John D. Lantos, James A. Tulsky (1996) Cardiopulmonary resuscitation on television: Miracles and Misinformation. *New England Journal of Medicine*, 334:1578–82.

Doherty, Mike (2012) 'Author Martin Amis on leaving England and finding America.' Online at www.macleans. ca, 6 September.

Dominiczak, Peter (2013) 'Mid-Staffs: Police investigating up to 300 deaths.' *Daily Telegraph*, 10 June.

Dwyer, Ciara (2012) 'The life and death of Josephine Hart.' *Irish Independent*, 30 November.

Dyer, Clare (2014) 'Doctors should consult patients before imposing non-resuscitation notices unless it would cause harm, Court of Appeal rules.' *British Medical Journal* 348:g4094 (17 June).

Ellershaw, J. E. and S. Wilkinson (eds) (2003) *Care of the Dying: a Pathway to Excellence*. Oxford: Oxford University Press.

Elsharkawy, Ahmed Mohamed and Mark Hudson (2012) 'The future developments in hepatology: no need for a jaundiced view.' *Frontline Gastroenterology*, 3(Supp 1):i47–i52.

Emanuel, Ezekiel J. (2014) 'Why I Hope to Die at 75.' *The Atlantic*, 17 September.

Emanuel, Ezekiel J. (2014) *Reinventing American Health Care*. New York: Public Affairs.

Evans, Jules (2012) *Philosophy for Life*. London: Random House.

Fisher, Lawrence (1999) 'The Race to Cash In On the Genetic Code.' *New York Times*, 29 August.

Fleming, Marie (with Sue Leonard) (2014) *An Act of Love*. Dublin: Hachette Books Ireland.

Foley, Michael (2010) *The Age of Absurdity: Why Modern Life Makes It Hard to Be Happy*. London: Simon & Schuster.

Freud, Sigmund (1915) 'Our attitude towards death,' in *Collected Papers*. London: Hogarth Press.

Fries, James F. (2005) 'The Compression of Morbidity.' *Milbank Q* 83(4):801–23.

Fritz, Zoë, Nick Cork, Alex Dodd, Alexandra Malyon (2014) 'DNACPR decisions: challenging and changing practice in the wake of the Tracey judgment.' *Clinical Medicine* 14(6):571–6.

Gawande, Atul (2010) 'Letting Go: What should medicine do when it can't save your life?' *New Yorker*, 2 August.

——(2014) *Being Mortal: Illness, Medicine, and What Matters in the End.* London: Profile Books.

Getz, L., A. L. Kirkengen, I. Hetlevik, S. Romundstad and J. A. Sigurdsson (2004) 'Ethical dilemmas arising from implementation of the European guidelines on cardio-vascular disease prevention in clinical practice.' *Scand J Prim Health Care* 22:202–208, December.

Gins, Madeline (2014) Obituary in the *Daily Telegraph*, 18 March.

Gorer, Geoffrey (1955) 'The Pornography of Death.' *Encounter*, October: 49–52.

——(1965) *Death, Grief and Mourning in Contemporary Britain.* London: Cresset Press.

Gould, Stephen Jay (1985) 'The Median Isn't the Message.' *Discover* 6 (June):46–9.

Gray, John (2002) *Straw Dogs: Thoughts on Humans and Other Animals.* London: Granta Books.

——(2011) *The Immortalization Commission: The Strange Quest to Cheat Death.* London: Allen Lane.

Grice, Elizabeth (2013) 'I was a desperate lover trying to save his love.' *Daily Telegraph*, 28 April.

Hall, Stephen S. (2010) 'Revolution Postponed.' *Scientific American*, October, 60–67.

Halpern, Scott D., George Loewenstein, Kevin G. Volpp, Elizabeth Cooney, Kelly Vranas, Caroline M. Quill, Mary S. McKenzie, Michael O. Hrhay, Nicole B. Gabler, Tatiana Silver, Robert Arnold, Derek C. Angus, Cindy Brice. 'Default Options in Advance Directives Influence How Patients Set Goals For End-Of-Life Care' (2013). *Health Affairs* 32(2):1–10.

Hamilton, Hugo (2014) *Every Single Minute*. London: Fourth Estate.

Hartocollis, Anemona (2009) 'At the End, Offering Not a Cure but Comfort.' *New York Times*, 19 August.

Hastings, Selina (2009) *The Secret Lives of Somerset Maugham*. London: John Murray.

Heath, Iona (2003) 'Ethical dilemmas in general practice: matters of life and death.' *Primary Care*, 3:942–7.

Hinton, John (1967) *Dying*. London: Penguin Books.

Hitchens, Christopher (2007) *God Is Not Great: The Case Against Religion*. London: Atlantic Books.

——(2010) *Hitch-22*. London: Atlantic Books.

——(2010) 'The New Commandments.' *Vanity Fair*, April.

——(2011) *The Quotable Hitchens: from Alcohol to Zionism*, edited by Windsor Mann. Cambridge, MA: Da Capo Press.

——(2012) *Mortality*. London: Atlantic Books.

Hoggart, Amy (2014) 'Simon Hoggart, my dad, was working, socialising and laughing to the end.' *Guardian*, 10 January.

Hook, Sidney (1987) 'In Defense of Voluntary Euthanasia.' *New York Times,* 1 March.

Hospice Friendly Hospitals (2010) *Quality Standards for End-of-Life Care in Hospitals.* Dublin: The Irish Hospice Foundation.

Illich, Ivan (1976) *Limits to Medicine: Medical Nemesis: The Expropriation of Health.* London: Penguin Books.

——(1994) 'Brave New Biocracy: Health Care from Womb to Tomb.' *New Perspectives Quarterly,* Winter, Vol. 11, Issue 1.

——(1995) 'Death undefeated.' *British Medical Journal,* 311:1652–3.

——(2002) Obituary in the *Times,* 5 December.

Iredale, John (2008) 'End-stage chronic liver disease: time to define a good death.' *Hepatology,* Vol. 47, Issue 6:1799–1800, June.

Irish Cancer Society (2013) *Towards a future without cancer.* Dublin: The Irish Cancer Society.

Jalland, Pat (2010) *Death in War and Peace: A History of Loss and Grief in England, 1914–1970.* Oxford: Oxford University Press.

Jangfeldt, Bengt (2008) *Axel Munthe: The Road to San Michele,* translated by Harry Watson. London: I. B. Tauris & Co.

Johnson, George (2013) *The Cancer Chronicles: Unlocking Medicine's Deepest Mystery.* London: The Bodley Head.

Jones, Steve (2009) 'One gene will not reveal all life's secrets.' *Daily Telegraph,* 20 April.

Jones, Toby (2012) 'Hitchens' last days', interview with Carol Blue. Australian Broadcasting Corporation.

Broadcast 25/11/12. Online at www.abc.net.au/lateline/content/2012/s3619164.htm

Kass, Leon R. (1997) 'The End of Courtship.' *Public Interest*, Winter issue.

——(2001) 'L'Chaim and Its Limits: Why Not Immortality?' *First Things*, May.

Kearney, Michael K., Radhule B. Weininger, Mary L. S. Vachon, Richard L. Harrison, Balfour M. Mount (2009) 'Self-care of Physicians Caring for Patients at the End of Life.' *Journal of the American Medical Association*, 301(11):1155–64.

Knowlson, James (1996) *Damned to Fame: The Life of Samuel Beckett*. London: Bloomsbury.

Kübler-Ross, Elisabeth (1969) *On Death and Dying*. London: Routledge.

Kurzweil, Ray (2005) *The Singularity Is Near: When Humans Transcend Biology*. New York: Viking.

Kurzweil, Ray and Terry Grossman (2009) *Transcend: Nine Steps to Living Well Forever*. New York: Rodale Books.

Lamas, Daniela J. (2013). 'If Your Heart Stopped Tonight'. *The Atlantic*, 25 October.

Lancet Oncology (editorial) (2015) 'Undermining the Hippocratic Oath: the Medical Innovation Bill.' *Lancet Oncology* 16:1.

Larkin, Philip (1988) *Collected Poems*, edited by Anthony Thwaite. London: Faber & Faber.

Levin, L. (2003) 'Ivan Illich: he lived his own testimony.' *Journal of Epidemiology & Community Health* 57:935.

Lewis, Jeremy (1998) *Cyril Connolly: A Life*. London: Pimlico.

Lucas, Viv (2012) '*The Death of Ivan Ilyich* and the concept of "total pain".' *Clinical Medicine*, Vol. 12. No. 6: 601–602.

MacClancy, Jeremy (2004) 'Geoffrey Gorer (1905–1985).' *Oxford Dictionary of National Biography*. Oxford: Oxford University Press.

Mann, Charles C. (2005) 'The Coming Death Shortage: Why the longevity boom will make us sorry to be alive.' *The Atlantic*, 1 May.

Marsh, Henry (2014) *Do No Harm: Stories of Life, Death and Brain Surgery*. London: Weidenfeld & Nicolson.

Maugham, W. Somerset (1938) *The Summing Up*. London: William Heinemann.

McGahern, John (2005) *Memoir*. London: Faber & Faber.

McPherson, Tess (2012) 'Personal View: My mum wanted assisted dying but we watched her die slowly and in pain.' *British Medical Journal*, 344:e4007.

Meek, James (2010) 'Some Wild Creature.' *London Review of Books*, Vol. 32, No. 14, 22 July.

Meyer, Harris (2010). First-year complications with assisted suicide. www. Crosscut.com/2010/03/firstyear-complications-with-assisted-suicide/

Miller, Franklin G. (2013) 'Two Philosophical Deaths: Hume and Hitchens.' *Perspectives in Biology and Medicine*, 56(2):251–8.

Mohammed, M. A., R. Lilford, G. Rudge, R. Holder and A. Stevens (2013) 'The findings of the Mid-Staffordshire

Inquiry do not uphold the use of hospital standardized mortality ratios as a screening test for "bad" hospitals.' *Quarterly Journal of Medicine*, 106:849–54.

Molloy, William (2005) *Let Me Decide.* Toronto: Penguin Books.

Moynihan, Ray and Richard Smith (2002) 'Too much medicine?' *British Medical Journal*, 324:859–60.

Munthe, Axel (1929) The Story of San Michele. London: John Murray.

Murray, Ken (2011) 'How Doctors Die.' Online at www.zocalopublicsquare.org, 30 November.

National end of life care intelligence network (2010) 'Death in Older Adults in England.' October. Online at www.endoflifecare-intelligence.org.uk.

Nisbet, Robert (1980) 'Death in the West.' Review of *The Hour of our Death* by Philippe Ariès. *New York Times*, 22 February.

Nuland, Sherwin B. (1994) *How We Die.* New York: Alfred A. Knopf.

O'Donnell, Michael (2010) 'Personal View: An unfortunate way to die.' *British Medical Journal*, 341:c5859, 20 October.

O' Faolain, Nuala (2008) 'I don't want more time. As soon as I heard I was going to die, the goodness went from life.' Interview in the *Irish Independent*, 13 April.

O'Mahony, Seamus (2013) 'The Big D'. Essay-length review of *Mortality* by Christopher Hitchens. *Dublin Review of Books*, Issue 41, 23 September.

——(2013) 'Against Narrative Medicine.' *Perspectives in Biology & Medicine*, 56(4):611–19.

——(2014) 'W. Somerset Maugham (1874–1965) and St Thomas' Hospital: Medical School and the making of a writer.' *Journal of Medical Biography*, 22:53–7.

——(2014) 'Axel Munthe and *The Story of San Michele*: The Perils of being a "Fashionable" Doctor.' *Clinical Medicine*, 14(3):321–2.

——(2015) 'Percutaneous Endoscopic Gastrostomy (PEG): cui bono?' *Frontline Gastroenterology* , 6:298–300.

O'Neill, Onora (2002) *A Question of Trust*. Cambridge: Cambridge University Press.

Oregon Public Health Division (2014). Oregon's Death with Dignity Act – 2014. www://public.health.oregon.gov/ ProviderPartnerResources/EvaluationResearch/Death withDignityAct/Documents/year17.pdf.

Orwell, George (1946) 'How the Poor Die' in *Decline of the English Murder and Other Essays*. London: Penguin (Penguin edn, 1965).

Ó Súilleabháin, Seán (1967) *Irish Wake Amusements* (translated by the author from the original Irish *Caitheamh Aimsire ar Thórraimh*, 1961). Cork: Mercier Press.

Parnia, Sam (with Josh Young) (2013) *The Lazarus Effect: The Science that is Rewriting the Boundaries Between Life and Death*. London: Rider.

Ponsky, Jeffrey L (2011). The Development of PEG: How it was. *Journal of Interventional Gastroenterology* 1:2,88–89.

Powell, J. Enoch (1966) *Medicine and Politics*. London: Pitman Medical.

Pyszczynski, Tom (2004) "What Are We So Afraid Of?" A Terror Management Theory Perspective on the Politics of Fear.' *Social Research*, 71(4):827–48.

Renault, Mary (1975) *The Nature of Alexander*. London: Allen Lane.

Richards, Mike and Claire Henry (2013) 'Liverpool Care Pathway: response to media reporting.' Online at www.endoflifecareforadults.nhs.uk.

Rieff, David (2005) 'Illness as More than Metaphor.' *New York Times Magazine*, 4 December.

Rieff, David (2008) *Swimming in a Sea of Death: A Son's Memoir*. London: Granta Books.

Rowe, Sam (2015) 'A dip in the gene pool.' *Daily Telegraph*, 27 June.

Royal College of Physicians, British Society of Gastro-enterology. (2010) *Oral feeding difficulties and dilemmas: a guide to practical care, particularly towards the end of life*. London: Royal College of Physicians.

Royal College of Physicians (2013) *Putting Patients First: Realising Francis' Vision*. London: Royal College of Physicians.

Royal College of Physicians, Marie Curie Cancer Care (2014) *National care of the dying audit for hospitals, England. National report*. London: Royal College of Physicians.

Saatchi, Maurice (2014) 'Cancer patients are dying because of our Downton Abbey treatment system.' *Guardian*, 14 November.

Saunders, Cicely (2006) *Selected Writings 1958–2002*, edited by Cicely Saunders and David Clark. Oxford: Oxford University Press.

Saunders, John (2013) 'Doctors and others: reflections on the first Francis Report.' *Clinical Medicine*, 13(2):132–5.

Scammell, Michael (2010) *Koestler: The Indispensable Intellectual*. London: Faber & Faber.

Scott, Caroline (2013) 'Locked In and Glad to be Alive.' *Sunday Times Magazine*, 16 June.

Sheehan, Maeve (2012) 'Mother who fought for cancer drug access dies.' *Irish Independent*, 29 July.

Smith, Rebecca (2014) 'Most terminally ill patients not told they are dying, says damning report.' *Daily Telegraph*, 14 May.

Smith, Richard (2012) 'The case for slow medicine.' *BMJ* blogs. Online at http://blogs.bmj.com/bmj/2012/12/17/richard-smith-the-case-for-slow-medicine/

——(2014) 'Dying of cancer is the best death.' Online at http://blogs.bmj.com/bmj/2014/12/31/richard-smith-dying-of-cancer-is-the-best-death/

Sullivan, Richard and the Lancet Oncology Commission (2011). 'Delivering affordable cancer care in high-income countries.' *Lancet Oncology*, 12:933–80.

Sweeney, Kieran, Liz Toy and Jocelyn Cornwell (2009) 'A patient's journey: Mesothelioma.' *British Medical* Journal, 339:b2862, 14 August.

Tallis, Raymond (2004) *Hippocratic Oaths: Medicine and its Discontents*. London: Atlantic Books.

——(2012) 'The case for assisted dying.' *New Humanist*, 16 August.

Tarleton, Yvonne (2013) 'Nobel winner's controversial views.' *Medical Independent*, 6 June.

Taylor, Paul (2013) 'Rigging the Death Rate.' *London Review of Books*, Vol. 35, No. 7, 11 April.

Temel, Jennifer S., Joseph A. Greer, Alona Muzikansky et al. (2010) 'Early Palliative Care for Patients with Metastatic Non-Small-Cell Lung Cancer.' *New England Journal of Medicine* 363:733–42, 19 August.

Thring, Oliver (2013) 'Diane, Debbie, my Tony… maybe the next one will win the right to die.' *Sunday Times*, 19 May.

Tolstoy, Leo (1886) *The Death of Ivan Ilyich & Other Stories*, translated by Peter Carson. London: Wordsworth Classics (2004).

Tsiompanou, Eleni, Caroline Lucas and Mike Stroud (2013) 'Overfeeding and overhydration in elderly medical patients: lessons from the Liverpool Care Pathway.' *Clinical Medicine*, Vol. 13, No. 3: 248–51, 1 June.

Wade, Nicholas (2010) 'A Decade Later, Genetic Map Yields few New Cures.' *New York Times*, 12 June.

Walsh, John (1999) *The Falling Angels: An Irish Romance*. London: HarperCollins.

Ware, Bronnie (2011) *The Top Five Regrets of the Dying: A Life Transformed by the Dearly Departing*. London: Hay House.

Waugh, Alexander (2004) *Fathers and Sons*. London: Headline Book Publishing.

Weiner, Jonathan (2010) *Long For This World: The Strange Science of Immortality.* New York: HarperCollins.

Wilson, A. N. (2006) *Betjeman.* London: Hutchinson.

Zuger, Abigail (2008) 'For the Very Old, a Dose of "Slow Medicine".' *New York Times,* 26 February.